5 EVERY MAN NEEDS

...And Every Woman Should Know About Men

Dwight Buckner, Jr.

5 THINGS EVERY MAN NEEDS

...And Every Woman Should Know About Men

Dwight Buckner, Jr.

T&J PUBLISHERS

A SMALL INDEPENDENT PUBLISHER WITH A BIG VOICE

Printed in the United States of America by
T&J Publishers (Atlanta, GA.)
www.TandJPublishers.com

© Copyright 2021 by Dwight Buckner, Jr.

All rights reserved. This book or parts thereof may not be reproduced in any form, stored in a retrieval system, or transmitted in any form by any means-electronic, mechanical, photocopy, recording, or otherwise-without prior written permission of the author, except as provided by United States of America copyright law.

All Bible verses are taken from the King James Version (KJV), New International Version (NIV), New Living Translation (NLT), and North American Standard Bible (NASB).

Cover Design by Timothy Flemming, Jr.
(T&J Publishers)
Book Format/Layout by Timothy Flemming, Jr.

ISBN: 978-1-7345105-9-1

To contact the author, go to:
PastorDwightBucknerJr.com
DwightBucknerJr@gmail.com
Facebook: Dwight Buckner Jr.
Instagram: Pastor Dwight Buckner Jr.
Twitter: Dwight Buckner Jr.
TikTok: Pastor Dwight Jr.

DEDICATIONS

First, I want to dedicate this book to my lovely wife, Elisa Buckner, and my two sons, Elias and Malachi Buckner. Thank you so much for your consistent love and support in everything God has called me to do. You guys are my number one fans.

I would also like to dedicate this book to every man and young boy. There are some great men out there. Just because we have made mistakes in the past does not mean we have to live in our mistakes. I pray men in particular would glean from the necessary tools implemented in this book.

Lastly, I would like to dedicate this book to every woman reading it. Thank you for taking time out to purchase this book so that you can understand the mind of a man. My prayer is for the men in your life to grow and thrive in what God has called them to do.

"Who can find a virtuous and capable wife?
She is more precious than rubies."—
Proverbs 31:10 (NLT)

TABLE OF CONTENTS

INTRO: YOU ARE THE KEY					11

CHAPTER 1: EVERY MAN NEEDS SUPPORT			15

CHAPTER 2: EVERY MAN NEEDS AFFIRMATION		39

CHAPTER 3: EVERY MAN NEEDS A SAFE PLACE		51

CHAPTER 4: EVERY MAN NEEDS SEX			71

CHAPTER 5: EVERY MAN NEEDS ACCOUNTABILITY	89

Intro | You Are The Key

HELLO, I AM SO GLAD YOU'VE DECIDED TO pick up this book. If you're holding this book in your hand, it's not by accident. There's no coincidence here. Something, or should I say, Someone drew you here. And not only did that special, supernatural Someone play a part in getting you here, but life's circumstances—they played a major role. You may be in a relationship with a man who's not fully living up to his potential or a man who's struggling to open up his heart to you; you might even be in a relationship with a man who's abusing you physically. Well, I can help you with the first two. That last one, all I can say is...RUN! Get out of that environment as fast as you can and let that man get the proper help he needs, and by "proper," I'm talking about the kind that comes through authorities and mental health experts. This book isn't designed for women who're in physically violent relationships or are dealing with partners who're battling addictions such as drugs or alcohol. This book is for the everyday relationships that face the typical—yet stressful—challenges of communication, trust and intimacy, the ones that may be on shaky ground due to unmet needs and expectations. I am here to help you, not merely adjust so that you can live with something substandard. No, God didn't design you just to exist or "just deal with it" when it comes to being in a relationship where you feel unhappy, emotionally disconnected, neglected or ignored. God didn't design you to live in misery. Sure, life is painful enough, but that is why God gave you a piece of Heaven wrapped up in what we know as an intimate relationship. In this type of relationship, you get to bond with someone who'll walk with you through the ups and downs of life, and you'll have a constant companion there to help you bear the burden of life's pains and disappointments. Not only that, but in this type of relationship, you'll find adventure as you embark upon a life of discovery and personal development with someone who's as mysterious as the universe above. God wants you to take the journey of life with someone that will fulfill your dreams and meet some of your deepest needs. And make no mistake, we all have deep needs and longings. I don't care how spiritual you are—Jesus is not and cannot be your boyfriend! He never assigned Himself that role. He gave that role to that special someone in your life, and my goal with this book is to help you and that special man in your life experience the happiness God desires for both of you. But first...

How do you get a man to be the type of man he

INTRO: YOU ARE THE KEY

was created to be? How do you get your man to open up and become more loving, more sensitive to your needs, to step into the kingly and priestly role in the household he was designed to walk in? How do you get him to be a loving husband, an open communicator? How? That's what I'm here to answer.

This book isn't the man-whisperer series. I'm not here to teach you tricks and tips that will help you manipulate a man into becoming what you want him to be. Instead, I am here to show you what a model relationship is supposed to look like according to the blueprint drawn by the One who created love, intimacy, and marriage: God. When you know what that design looks like, you'll be able to make the necessary changes in yourself that will have a domino effect in your relationship, triggering a change in your mate. You will be able to let go of hurt, pain, and bitterness caused by unrealistic and unfair expectations and operate in a spirit of love and forgiveness, which are the necessary ingredients that cause every relationship to grow and thrive. Furthermore, when you discover the power you possess as a woman, you will understand why I decided to focus on helping women first to improve and grow wonderful marriages and relationships. The woman is the key. Trust me. It's true.

Don't worry. I have some excellent advice for men in this book. And I do have a book that's dedicated just for men coming down the pipeline as well. But for now, this book is for you. It's time for you, as a woman, to discover the power you have and experience the happiness you deserve. That's why you picked up this book—why God led you to this book. So I'm ready if you are. Let's get started.

1 | Every Man Needs Support

IN 1958, GABRIEL GARCIA MARQUEZ SAW A beautiful girl on the dance floor at their grade school dance; her name was Mercedes Barcha Pardo. Although she was only thirteen-years-old and Gabriel was sixteen, it was love at first sight. Later that year, Gabriel proposed to her, but her parents wanted her to finish grade school before getting married, which she did.

Thirteen years after he proposed to her, Gabriel and Mercedes got married. That was the happiest day of their lives, but it was also the beginning of a long journey. Gabriel's goal in life was to become a writer. At the time, he was enrolled in law school pursuing a law degree in order to please his father; however, practicing law was not his dream; it wasn't his passion. Sure, practicing law would have provided a sense of comfort and financial stability. The many people around him would have been pleased, but he would have been miserable. There was a burning, aching desire in him to write, and nothing could shake it. Although Gabriel and his wife, Mercedes, were poor, this didn't diminish the dream he had on the inside of him. Also, Mercedes believed in his dream.

Mercedes not only believed in her husband's dream; she encouraged him to pursue it. She told him to focus on writing his novel while she worked. For a while, she became the breadwinner. She did everything in her power to take the stress off of her husband so that he could focus. This didn't look good to some people. There were those who questioned her decision to work while her husband followed his dream. Some people called her foolish and delusional and accused her of enabling a man who was a fool. However, several months later, his dream became a reality. He finished his first novel, *One Hundred Years of Solitude*, which became an instant classic. He'd soon become one of the most successful and highly acclaimed authors in the world, and go on to receive the Nobel Prize in literature.

What if Mercedes would have discouraged her husband from pursuing his dream? What if she would have berated and belittled him for thinking he could get anywhere in life with his writings? What if she would have torn her husband down rather than build him up with her words? What if she had encouraged him to go back to law school rather than pursue his goal of becoming a novelist? They would have forfeited the life of their dreams.

There have been great men throughout history that accomplished incredible feats. We talk about men like Dr. Martin Luther King, Jr., Winston Churchill, Abra-

CHAPTER 1: EVERY MAN NEEDS SUPPORT

ham Lincoln, and other world-shakers, but we forget that the source of these men's strength and courage were the powerful women in their lives. Had Coretta discouraged Martin rather than encouraging him to pursue his goal of being a civil rights activist, the Civil Rights Movement would have incurred a great loss, one that might have set the movement back years or even decades.

I remember hearing actor and playwright, Tyler Perry, share his testimony about his path to success. He talked about the dream God placed inside of him to write plays. Of course, the only woman in his life at the time was his mother. The advice she gave him was far from encouraging. She told him to give up his dream of becoming a playwright and get a job at the telephone company. Thank God, Tyler Perry didn't follow his mother's advice—and she's glad he didn't either. Had he listened to her discouraging advice, he'd currently be working for the telephone company, making around forty-thousand dollars a year as opposed to operating his own movie studio and raking in millions of dollars.

Let me ask you a question: Are you married to the next Gabriel Marquez and don't know it? Are you engaged to the next Dr. King, Jr. and don't realize it? Are you completely oblivious of the true potential and destiny your man has? Do you know what you have in your possession in the form of that man? He's more than just a man; he's a carrier of great potential, a specimen created with a divine destiny slated for greatness. He may not look like it now; in fact, he may appear to be the opposite of what I'm proposing to you, but that doesn't negate the fact that he possesses within him some gift or ability that, if recognized and tapped into, can not only produce the life of your dreams, but change the world.

In most cases, that man may never know what's on the inside of him if you don't help him to discover it. This leads me to my next point—

THE BIGGEST ROLE

God has a plan for couples to build His Kingdom, to be prosperous, and to leave a lasting legacy, but the successful execution of this plan for our families depends on our ability to submit to His order for the family. If we will do our parts (and make no doubt about it, we all have a part to play), then we will experience blessings and the life of our dreams just like the men I mentioned above. And ladies, let me assure you of one thing: the biggest role is the one you play.

When I read the Bible, I notice that a lot of responsibility is actually given to women to determine the success or failure of a home. Sounds odd, I know. In fact, that runs counter to what's often taught in churches across this nation. We often claim the men are responsible for the success of the home, but that's not the case. Men succeed because they have the right support; therefore, it's not the man, but the one who supports the man that plays the biggest role in determining the success or failure of the household.

Listen to what King Solomon shared with us in the book of Proverbs about the power of women in the home:

> "A wise woman builds her home, but a foolish woman tears it down with her own hands." (14:1,

CHAPTER 1: EVERY MAN NEEDS SUPPORT

NLT)

The burden of responsibility the woman carries is building the house. What that means is the man may provide a house, but the woman is the one who provides a home; she's the one who makes that home a place of nourishment and revitalization or a place of discouragement and devitalization. She provides what her man needs to become who God has predestined him to be, but she can also be the biggest hindrance to the success of the home; it all depends on her words, actions, and deeds.

Solomon further noted: "By wisdom a house is built and by understanding it is established" (Proverbs 24:3, NLT). Here's a basic definition of wisdom: *Doing things God's way as opposed to the world's way.* That's it in a nutshell. God's way guarantees success. On the other hand, our way guarantees failure. Doing relationships God's way allows our marriages to thrive and our households to experience blessings and prosperity. I'm sure that's what you want. I believe this is what everyone wants. However, to receive this, we need God's wisdom.

It is for this reason that Solomon ranked the value and worth of a wise wife far above the most valuable, rare, and precious jewels. He said, "Who can find a virtuous wife? For her worth is far above rubies" (Proverbs 31:10, NKJV). That means, should a man have to choose between having all of the money in the world and having a wise wife, the wise wife would be far more valuable. She's resourceful, her lips are full of praise and encouragement, she lifts her husband's spirit and affects him on a level money and material possessions can never do. She is invaluable. She's priceless. He'd be right in asking, "What would I do without her?"

A woman full of God's wisdom will make her house a home where hopes and dreams can grow and flourish; she will transform it into a place where godly ideas can be incubated. This kind of woman will turn her home into a charging station where not only her man, but her children can be recharged and gain fresh strength and energy to pursue the plans and the purposes of God for their lives. And no, she's not left out in the cold. By serving her husband and helping him to arrive at where he needs to be, she's also positioning herself to experience the personal hopes and dreams embedded in her own heart. Let me explain.

BUILDING THE VISION

When God created mankind in the Garden of Eden, He established an order. He created Adam first. Upon creating Adam, He instructed Adam to tend to the garden and name every species of creature on the earth. God didn't merely give Adam a job; He gave Adam a vision. A vision is different from a job in that visions align with one's purposes in life; they also create generational wealth and prosperity, and cannot be accomplished without help. Visions stem from the inside out, not the outside in. Sam Walton had a vision, which was to create a retail store that would offer great quality products at a very low cost. He founded Walmart, but he didn't do it by himself. Walmart is a family-owned business. Sam's wife, Helen, helped him build their retail store empire (Walmart and Sam's Club), which, as of the year 2020, earns the Walton family four

CHAPTER 1: EVERY MAN NEEDS SUPPORT

million dollars per hour. The founder of Hobby Lobby, David Green, had a vision to create a chain of arts and craft stores. His vision was too big for him to pull off alone, so he enlisted the help of his family, starting with his wife, Barbara, who came alongside him and helped to build his vision. Today, the Green family is worth billions.

I'm sure you get the point by now. God built men in a special way. He designed men to be visionaries, to be leaders. Adam came fully loaded. He came with all of the gifts, talents, and potential already inside of him. In fact, he was created grown—he didn't have to grow up and learn like the rest of us. So, you'd think that Adam was sufficient by himself and was equipped to accomplish God's assignment for his life alone, but that was not the case. It was God who looked at Adam and noticed that there was something missing from his life. God looked and saw that Adam was alone, and then uttered those famous words: "It is not good for the man to be alone. I will make a helper who is just right for him" (Genesis 2:18, NLT). He realized that He placed a heavy load on Adam, one that not only consisted of tending to the garden, but also entailed populating the earth. Adam wouldn't have been able to accomplish these tasks alone, so God created Eve—she was to be Adam's helper.

Eve complimented Adam in every way. She not only complimented him physically, but also spiritually. She was especially suited to help Adam accomplish the mission for which he was created. She came loaded with the tools he needed to fulfill the assignment that was on his life. Ladies, let me stop and say this: When God matches you with a man (notice I said 'when God' does it, not you), He aligns you with a man whose purpose requires your talents and gifts. There is something special inside of that man, just as there is something special on the inside of you. You are spiritually compatible before anything else. You have what he needs. He has an assignment on his life that requires your help, one that will benefit you and your children, establishing generational wealth and prosperity. The two of you must become a team, not just lovers. You must create together and build your empire together. He's supposed to be your king, and you're supposed to be his queen. That's what God has in mind, which is why it's critical that you (1) let God direct you to the right man, (2) you discover that man's vision, and (3) you discover what talents and gifts God has given you to facilitate that vision. Both of you were created by God for a singular purpose that will feed your individual goals. Helen Walton went on to birth several other foundations and organizations and followed her own philanthropic ambitions, but the funding for her personal dreams came from her husband's vision. The same can also be said about the wives of every other visionary throughout history who succeeded. When you help the man that God gave you accomplish the vision God gave him, you will find yourself in the position to carry out the personal plans in your heart without struggling. Actually, this is emphasized in what Bible scholars call the "law of stewardship" found in Luke 16:10-12, which says,

> "If you are faithful in little things, you will be faithful in large ones. But if you are dishonest in little things, you won't be honest with greater re-

CHAPTER 1: EVERY MAN NEEDS SUPPORT

sponsibilities. And if you are untrustworthy about worldly wealth, who will trust you with the true riches of heaven? **And if you are not faithful with other people's things, why should you be trusted with things of your own?**" (NLT)

The principle found here states when we serve others, God will in-turn cause others to serve us. When we bless others to achieve their goals, God will send people into our lives to help us achieve our goals. What we make happen for others, God will make happen for us. It is important that we don't become selfish and insecure and think that serving another person will cause us to miss our blessings and opportunities to shine. Actually, by serving others, we are sowing positive seeds that will come back to bless us up the road. God is the strategist, and He's trying to bless you and your man beyond your wildest dreams.

Remember: Building your man means building his vision. As Coretta Scott King once stated: "What most did not understand then was that I was not only married to the man I loved, but I was also married to the movement that I loved." Coretta married Martin's vision, and helped him to fulfill it. Without her, he wouldn't have succeeded in such an undertaking.

Now, you may be thinking, *That sounds good, but my husband doesn't have a vision. He doesn't want to do anything with his life.* First, let me inform you that every man possesses the potential to be a king, and developing a vision usually takes time. As men mature, they begin to think more about creating a legacy; their focuses shift from thinking about themselves to thinking about the lasting impression they are going to leave behind and what other people will remember them for. That's why they invest so much into their children, hoping that they will not only benefit from their hard work, but take what they've left to them to another level. So sometimes, a man doesn't come to the place of recognizing the need for a vision until later on in life, but once he becomes motivated by a sense of vision, that's when you'll see a difference in his goals and behavior.

Furthermore, developing a vision isn't simply the result of age and mental maturity; it is also the result of necessity and internal discovery. Some men have yet to discover their true potentials and purposes, but with the right aid and assistance, they can make this discovery; this depends, however, on the company they keep. Being around other successful people tends to spark an interest in us to be successful. Being around goal-oriented people causes us to think about our goals. And most importantly, when a man has a woman who encourages him to be more than what he is, using the power of encouragement to transform his perspective of life and of himself, this can bring out the best in him; this can cause him to dig deep within to find a vision so that he can create a better life of himself and his family.

Ladies, let me let you in on a little secret: A man's true motivation for creating a vision is never for himself; it's always for his family. He's always thinking about how he can provide the best for his woman and for his children. Men have pride. What strengthens their sense of pride is being good providers and strong protectors. Men feel like men when they're protecting their women and

CHAPTER 1: EVERY MAN NEEDS SUPPORT

kids, and they feel like men when they're providing for their families. That is why most men never really request anything for Father's Day; they just enjoy seeing the smiles on their wives' and children's faces. That's their gift. Not the tie and socks you buy them every year. So when you help a man to discover his potential and worth and build his vision, he will fall even more in love with you. There's nothing more powerful than a motivated man. Nothing on this earth, that is. And encouragement is the key ingredient in building a motivated man.

WHY HE NEEDS A CHEERLEADER

Whenever watching football or basketball, most people only notice the players on the field or on the court; however, very few people notice "the team behind the team": the cheerleaders. There's a good reason why cheerleaders exist. They boost the spirits and the morale of the players on the field and on the court; they also raise the energy of the audience in the stands. This activity has unseen effects on the game. Unknowingly, players feed on the audience's energy. The crowd's energy boosts the players' energy, and many times, it's that additional boost of energy that gives the players the edge they need to overcome the drag they may feel and finish the game, and even win the game.

Being a cheerleader is the same as being an encourager. To encourage means "to give confidence and hope to; to give support and advice to so that someone will do or continue to do something; to help or stimulate an activity, state, or view to develop." So, by cheering your man on, you're giving him a greater sense of confidence, providing him with a sense of hope, and giving him the strength to do something he is afraid to do or continue to do when he wants to quit out of fear and frustration. Your encouragement energizes your man, giving him the ability to go the extra mile.

There's a misconception out there about men. Many women believe men don't need encouragement. They think men never get weak or become frightened. I'll admit that much of this perception is attributed to men's tendency to hide their fears and vulnerabilities. Boys are usually taught that being emotional is a sign of weakness and that "a man" must always appear strong, and this false teaching doesn't only affect men, it also affects leaders in every industry and field. People are told that if they're in leadership (whether in ministry, business, or in any other industry), they cannot allow others to *see them sweat*; they must maintain the *appearance* of being in control at all times. And to be honest, if the leader of your ministry of business is freaking out all of the time, this can lower your morale and sense of confidence. Yes, people do gain courage from the strength of their leaders; they're inspired by their leaders' display of tenacity and boldness. That's why we hail heroes in our society.

But where do the heroes go to rejuvenate and regain their strength?

Great leaders need great support systems in order to stay the course; likewise, men need encouragers to remain on the battlefield of life and deal with the stress of work and the crippling pressures of life. Men have a lot to think about. They often worry about how they're going to provide for their families, how they're going to protect their families, and they're under a tremendous amount of

CHAPTER 1: EVERY MAN NEEDS SUPPORT

pressure to lead their households. With so much on their shoulders, men easily grow frustrated and get weak. And I'm simply talking about a man's domestic duties; I haven't even discussed his higher purpose, which could consist of challenging an entire culture as Dr. King, Jr. and Ghanda did. He may be fearful of starting that business for fear of faillure despite knowing he should. Your encouragement can give him the energy and strength he needs to do what must be done.

Most men have never learned how to process their emotions. Again, most of them were taught to ignore their emotions. However, emotions are a part of human nature. Everyone experiences hurt, pain, disappointment, frustration, fear, anxiety, anger, guilt, shame, disgust, happiness, sadness, and more. Men specialize in creating tough exteriors while masking these emotions. And they're usually not going to tell you when they're scared—they were told that if a woman sees a man displaying the emotion of fear, she'll lose respect for him; she'll doubt his ability to be a strong, brave and courageous protector, and will move on to the next man. So, he hides his fear, he hides his frustration and anxiety, and pretends to be braver than he really is. It's a vicious cycle of self-sabotage. For Example, when a husband fails to lower his facade and ask for help from his woman, he allows the weight and pressure he feels to crush him further. He suffers in silence until he can't go on. That's why encouragement from his woman is more important than encouragement from someone else. When a wife encourages her husband, she relieves him of a pressure she didn't know he had: the pressure to impress her with a facade. She unconsciously communicates to him

27

that he doesn't have to worry about losing her if he shows vulnerability. He feels empowered now, knowing he's not alone and no longer needs to pretend to be something he's not: invulnerable.

Her act of encouragement is really a recognition of his human nature. The strong don't need encouragement; only the weak need encouragement. Those who lack vulnerabilities don't need someone to come alongside them and help them carry the load of responsibility; only those who aren't self-reliant need a partner to get things done in life. The inner, hidden man lurking inside of him who's silently screaming for the love and support of another secretly feels rescued by the woman who can see past his tough exterior and see his true condition and hear his silent cries. She dissolves his fears and disarms him, causing him to perceive her as invaluable. She is even providing a need that others have deprived him of in his life. Maybe his dad never wrapped his arms around him and said the words "I believe in you" and "I'm proud of you". Perhaps his mother rebuffed him when he approached her for emotional support. Now, his wife is unknowingly healing his childhood wounds by providing him with the very validation he failed to receive as a boy.

A woman can make a man feel like he can conquer the world through encouragement. Encouragement not only heals your man's hidden wounds, but it establishes a greater level of trust and intimacy between the two of you, and this strong emotional bond can protect your relationship from outside influences and destructive affairs.

The world would have us to believe that men solely desire sexual fulfillment, as if they don't possess emotion-

CHAPTER 1: EVERY MAN NEEDS SUPPORT

al needs. Men want to feel desired. They long to feel needed. They want someone to be a source of encouragement in their lives: a woman to say, "I believe in you." However, when he's not getting this at home, he becomes vulnerable to seduction from other women. Intimacy fuels the fire of sexual attraction, and what breeds intimacy is a strong emotional connection. Like a moth drawn to a flame, men are drawn to supportive women who offer them encouragement, thereby fulfilling their emotional need.

You probably didn't think simple words of encouragement meant so much to a man. I can assure you they do. Psychologists will tell you the same thing. In an article entitled *The Quiet Power of Encouragement* written in Psychology Today, Julie J. Exline, Ph.D., explained,

> "...what an amazing gift we can offer to others through encouragement! When we "en-courage," it's as though we actually infuse courage into another person. Encouragement can provide people with strength to look ahead, move forward, and reach for the next goal. The whole emotional tone of a tough situation can be transformed through encouragement. Somehow things seem a little brighter."

She reveals to readers that there's a tendency to feel a sense of shame whenever someone fails at a task or a goal, and that an act of encouragement in its many forms (from a "soft smile, a kind word, or a light touch on the hand" to "lavish and effusive praise, bear hugs, and hearty cheers or applause") can transform their perspective of the situation and prevent them from becoming mentally and emotionally scarred due to things not going their way.

THE MAGIC RULE IN COMMUNICATION

Dr. John Gottman is recognized as the foremost authority in the field of relationship counseling. He predicted the success and failure of couples with 90% accuracy. Through his many decades of marriage and relationship counseling, he discovered what he called The Four Horsemen of the Apocalypse in Marriage (the reference to the Four Horsemen of the Apocalypse is based on the book of Revelation in the Bible, and it highlights the four events that will occur during the last days and the final judgment of God upon the earth). Gottman's four horsemen are signs that a marriage is heading towards the divorce court. At the very top of the list, the very first horsemen to watch out for, is criticism. His research reveals that when a couple begins to criticize one another, their relationship is in grave danger and is on the verge of splitting up.

What is criticism? It's defined as "the expression of disapproval of someone or something based on perceived faults or mistakes" (Dictionary.com). In other words, *criticism* is the act of constantly pointing out someone's faults, failures, weaknesses and shortcomings, and reminding them of how displeased you are because of these things. You tend only to focus on a person's wrongs whenever you talk to them.

Some women believe that by criticizing their husbands and boyfriends, they will motivate them to change; however, it's the opposite that happens. Criticism beats a man down and causes him to become more defensive.

CHAPTER 1: EVERY MAN NEEDS SUPPORT

Criticism makes people feel like nothing they do is good enough, like they are failures, and like they are unappreciated. To preserve his ego, sense of pride and self-esteem, a man will usually respond with anger, resentment, and resistance. You cannot criticize someone into meeting your needs and making positive changes, especially since criticism only causes others resent you and avoid doing the very thing you want them to do out of spitefulness.

No one wants to be controlled by another person. When people serve others, they do so out of love, not fear or coercion. Some people believe criticism motivates others. It doesn't. Criticism is perceived as, and rightfully so, a form of mental manipulation, and such an action only brings about the opposite of what you desire and expect.

There is a type of criticism called *constructive criticism*, which is "a helpful way of giving feedback that provides specific, actionable suggestions" (indeed.com). The main emphasis is on being positive and giving solutions, not simply pointing out what you don't like in a negative and harsh manner while offering no solutions. *How* you speak to someone, especially a man who is, by nature, fueled by his ego and pride and whose mega need is honor and respect, is just as important as *what* you say to them. Make a man feel like he's being attacked and he will go into defense mode. Make him feel appreciated and respected and he will be open to any suggestions you have that will help him be a better husband, father, and more. It's all about *how* you start the conversation.

Proverbs 16:24 says, "Kind words are like honey—sweet to the soul and healthy for the body" (NLT). Genuine compliments and praises are "kind words" that diffuse tensions in relationships and disarm people. In fact, kind words make the other person feel validated and appreciated. When you acknowledge the good a person has done first and cause them to feel appreciated, they'll be more willing to hear any criticism you have to offer. Just remember the first and most important rule: make your man feel as if you appreciate him by acknowledging the things he's done—by acknowledging his positive contributions, strengths, attributes, and actions. Take some time to think about what he's done right and bring it up before you bring up what you don't like and want him to do differently.

The Gottman Institute shared the rule for offering criticism. In an article entitled *The Magic Relationship Ratio, According To Science*, they stated, "That 'magic ratio' is 5 to 1. This means that for every negative interaction during conflict, a stable and happy marriage has five (or more) positive interactions." So for every one criticism you give to someone, you need to give five or more compliments. Lead the conversation with positive words and this will bring a more desirable outcome. Your man will listen more, and value your feedback. Your critique of him and his ways and actions won't make him feel attacked and discouraged.

Think about it. Would you go up to someone you greatly admire and look up to and criticize them? If you are interviewing for a job, would you upon first meeting your potential employer criticize how they look or sound? Or would you toss a compliment their way at the start of the interview? You already know what others will think of you if you start a conversation with criticism rather than

CHAPTER 1: EVERY MAN NEEDS SUPPORT

praise. Why then would it be any different with your relationship? If you and your beau are no longer friends, most likely, it's because you and your partner are trapped in a cycle of fault-finding, thereby making each other feel unworthy and judged. The solution to this problem is simple: think back to how you first became friends. You became friends due to positive words; so to become friends again, get back to speaking positive words to one another. Do what you did when you first met and you will feel that emotional connection return to your relationship.

WHAT ENCOURAGEMENT LOOKS LIKE TO A MAN

Now that we've gotten that out of the way, here's where I get practical. This is where I lay it all out for you, revealing what support looks and sounds like to a man.

Let him lead

In every organization there is a structure that allows it to function properly. Everyone is assigned different roles and responsibilities. No one is trying to do another person's job. The same is to be said regarding marriage: everyone has a role and a responsibility. When couples abandon their assigned roles, dysfunction arises. This is why society is filled with so many dysfunctional families—no one knows what they're supposed to do.

Done God's way, the man is supposed to be the head of the household. 1 Corinthians 11:3 says, "But there is one thing I want you to know: The head of every man is Christ, the head of woman is man, and the head of Christ is God" (NLT). So the man is supposed to be the head, which means he's the leader. Easier said than done. Many men struggle with taking the lead in their households, forgetting the cardinal rule the Bible gives us here: *He can't lead his family if he isn't being led by Christ.* Therefore, his role as a leader begins with his spiritual life and walk with God. He is tasked by God with praying over his family, speaking destiny over his children, covering his wife in prayer as the priest of the home, receiving instructions from God on where to lead the family and then communicating those instructions to the rest of the household. Sadly, many women are in relationships with men who don't know how to lead God's way, and they get frustrated and begin to assume the role of the leader within the home. But only emasculates the man and discourages him from being the leader he's supposed to be. The more the woman takes the lead, the more emasculated he becomes, until he eventually retreats and abandons his responsibility altogether.

This might not be comforting news, but most men have to be encouraged into the role of spiritual leader in the home. For example, statistics reveal that more women attend church than men across the nation. One reason for this, according to researchers, is that many houses of worship fail to appeal to men. Many churches offer programs that cater mainly to women; promote a message of passivity, which most men can't relate to; and often lack masculine role models.

The Bible tells us that a woman who honors and respects her husband, accepting his position as the leader rather than fighting him, constantly opposing him, being combative, acting disrespectfully towards him, and un-

CHAPTER 1: EVERY MAN NEEDS SUPPORT

dermining his authority in the home, will win over even a sinful husband; he will see the fruit of God's Spirit in her life, which is manifested as a quiet and gentle spirit. That means she is supportive, positive, kind, tender, and cooperative. No, this doesn't mean she's a doormat—she has standards and moral values and refuses to do that which is a blatant contradiction of what she knows to be right. However, she's submissive enough to let her husband lead, even if she's the more capable one. She practices humility in the face of her husband, which, in turn, makes him feel empowered and more appreciative of her. And it's because of her gentle spirit that her husband feels calm and relaxed around her and in the home.

Your man may not attend church and listen to a preacher, but he will listen to your lifestyle. He'll become more interested in the God you serve when he notices how your faith has caused a change in your behavior towards him. When you go from quarrelsome to cooperative and supportive because of the conviction of the Holy Spirit in your life, this change in you will spark a spiritual awakening inside of him as indicated in 1 Peter 3:1-5.

**Show him you trust him,
and don't try to do things for him**

It's important that you verbally communicate to your man that you respect his decisions and his leadership even if you don't agree with all of his decisions. You encourage him to lead by choosing to let him step up and take the initiative in the relationship. And again, the key isn't to criticize him into doing this, but to encourage him with positive words.

If there's something you need him to do or want him to do, or there is something he forgot to do but needs to do, kindly remind him and hold him accountable; don't go and do it for him. If the car needs to be fixed, don't call your cousin over to fix it; let your man focus on getting it fixed. Remind him and encourage him, and then let him do it. By bringing in another person to do what he is supposed to do without first consulting with him is a way of telling him you don't believe in his ability to lead and that you think he's incompetent. By jumping up and doing it yourself, you're telling your man you don't think he's capable. He sees this as you not believing in him. He needs to develop a sense of pride through accomplishment, and if you take that opportunity away from him, his ego and self-esteem will take a hit, and this will only lead to more discouragement and less motivation to do the things that must be done. He wants to show you that he can provide and protect you, so let him do it.

Tell him you believe in him
As we covered earlier, it is so important that you communicate to your man that you believe in him. When a man knows that his woman believes in him, he will develop the confidence and the motivation to conquer the world…on her behalf. Hearing those magic words "Baby, I believe in you" will light a fire under your man like nothing else and empower him to keep going. That is the main cheer your man needs to hear.

Express to him and show him that you have his back
As stated earlier, your man needs to know that you be-

CHAPTER 1: EVERY MAN NEEDS SUPPORT

lieve in him and that he can rely on you. Knowing that you are in his corner will boost his confidence. He knows he's not alone, that he has someone to watch his back and will roll up their sleeves and get in the mud with him. But showing your man you have his back means being by his side and on his side. So never esteem the opinions of others over your man, and don't put your family and friends in front of him. They may talk negatively about your man, but that's where draw the line. You have to decide whether or not defending your man's honor—and your decision to be with him—is worth it. Furthermore, it's important that you don't share your man's secrets with others. Don't talk about his imperfections with your girlfriends or discuss what you don't like about him with your family. Keep out all outsiders besides a trusted, spiritual confidant or professional. Failure to do this will violate the sacredness of your relationship and cause your man to distrust you.

Express appreciation for the things he does for you and your home

In psychology, there's something called positive reinforcement. With this, you praise a child or individual whenever they do something you want them to do. By praising a certain behavior, you motivate them to do it more. If you praise your man for taking out the trash, he'll do it more because he knows it pleases you and because he enjoys the praises you heap on him for doing it. Identify the behaviors your man is engaging in that are good and acknowledge and praise those behaviors. Don't ignore him when he does them or you will send him the message that those behaviors don't matter to you. Express appreciation more for what he does for you and he will do it more.

Show interest in him

Another way to show your man support is to give him your undivided attention. In a world full of distractions, the simple art of communicating effectively has been lost. People don't know how to engage in a conversation that's not filled with emojis. People don't know how to put away gadgets and look one another in the eyes and simply talk. However, if you are going to build a strong relationship, you must make time for one another, and this entails carving out time that is gadget-free so that you can hear each other. When staring at your phone, fumbling with the remote control, pecking away at your computer, reading a book, and doing other activities while your partner is communicating with you, the message you are communicating to them at that moment is, "You are not interesting to me. I am not interested in what you have to say." If your man feels like you're not interested in him, he won't feel like you're supportive of him. And why should he? He thinks he's not even worth a moment of your time.

2 | Every Man Needs Affirmation

I HUG AND KISS MY SONS EVERY DAY. Of course, it irritates them and gets on their nerves; at least, that's how they make it seem. But I don't care. As big as they are, as masculine as they are, it doesn't matter.

In my journey from childhood to manhood, I discovered the importance of affirming the people you love. When we are children, we don't realize we need it. Then, when we become teenagers, we forget or pretend like we don't need it. But when we grow up, we recognize the importance of being affirmed, and we can realize the consequences of not being affirmed by those we love.

What does it mean to affirm someone? The word *affirm* means "state as a fact; to assert strongly and publicly; to accept or confirm the validity of." So when affirming something, you're publicly claiming that it is real, valid, and authentic; in essence, you're offering your approval of something.

That's basically what an affirmation is: your verbal declaration of approval of someone or something. What I longed for as a boy was for my father to tell me he approved of me, and as crazy as this might sound, I longed for him to say those words and publicly confirm my identity as a man even after I became an adult.

There's power in an affirmation. Cultures around the world understand this. But unfortunately, many within our society today do not. For example, when boys reach twelve in the Jewish community, their families will throw a Bar mitzvah. During this coming-of-age celebration, they acknowledge the boys' transition from childhood to manhood. They do the same for girls; theirs is called a Bat mitzvah. In Ethiopia, one tribe—the Hamar Tribe—has an interesting coming-of-age ceremony: Boys must jump over a row of bulls four times during a three-day ritual; this initiates the boys' transition into manhood. And then, some coming-of-age rituals are really strange, such as the one found in Brazil among a tribe in the Amazon. There, 13-year-old boys must harvest bullet ants (they are called this because the pain from these giant ants' stings is comparable to that of being shot with a gun). Next, they must weave these ants into gloves with the stingers facing inward and then wear these gloves multiple times for several minutes each day. Ouch! And they are not allowed to show any pain.

All over the world, cultures engage in some practice that essentially affirms the passage of young boys and girls into manhood or womanhood. For example, when a girl's menstrual cycle first comes on, many parents will

CHAPTER 2: EVERY MAN NEEDS AFFIRMATION

hold a menstrual party/celebration for the girl; this is a way of minimizing the girl's fear and anxiety and affirming that she's entered into a phase of adult maturity. She's being told that she's now becoming a woman. She feels a sense of pride resulting from this affirmation, realizing there's nothing wrong with her and that her menstrual cycle is perfectly normal.

This point may be more for the men, but ladies, this will help you understand much of the cause behind your man's behavior and how to help him become the man he's supposed to be. Men need other men, specifically a father figure, to affirm them. Women can't affirm men. He needs a father to teach him how to be a man and confirm his passage into manhood officially. This confirmation will boost his pride and solidify in his mind that he's an authentic man, that he's passed the test of approval by a real man. Without this approval and acceptance, he will wander in the wilderness of confusion, never sure if he adds up or not. Unfortunately, for many boys who don't have a father in the home to affirm them, they turn to the streets to find father figures, and the thugs and dope boys usually step in and fill the void in their lives. If a thug or dope dealer is now the standard for a boy, think about what that means. Single mothers need to introduce their sons to positive adult male role models like sports coaches, pastors, and other similar figures so that they can have positive standards to live up to.

The reality is, sometimes, we receive the most support from people outside the home. One example of this was King David. His father, Jesse, refused to affirm him as a son. Jesse treated David like he didn't even exist. He gave

David's brothers all of the attention they needed, though. He didn't see what God had placed inside of David; he didn't know he had a king in his midst. David didn't look like much, but God sent others to affirm him. God sent the prophet Samuel to affirm David, anointing him as Israel's next king. God sent King Saul to affirm David, taking David under his wings. God even sent Saul's son, Jonathan, to affirm David, recognizing the greatness on David's life and becoming the friend and brother David never had. So we must remember that God knows the need for affirmation, and He will send people to affirm us, even from outside of the home. Don't rely on the people in your own house for affirmation because your greatest support system may come from somewhere else.

Their fathers have never affirmed many young men; some have never received an affirmation, even from a father figure; this creates a situation where a man may grapple with his sense of identity. Many women find themselves being innocent bystanders watching their men engage in these silent wars, battling depression and feelings of emptiness. They tend to feel helpless, longing to rescue their men. But here's where wisdom kicks in.

THE POWER OF UNDERSTANDING

The Bible says, "Wisdom is the principal thing; therefore get wisdom: and with all thy getting get understanding" (Proverbs 4:7, KJV). I prefer the way the New Living Translation puts it: "Getting wisdom is the wisest thing you can do! And whatever else you do, develop good judgment." Getting wisdom and understanding means you must increase in knowledge to know what's going on and

CHAPTER 2: EVERY MAN NEEDS AFFIRMATION

why a person is the way they are. So don't just get up and yell at someone for being a certain way; seek to know why they're the way they are and then learn the appropriate way of aiding and assisting them to recovery.

Many men struggle with depression, loneliness and a sense of emptiness. These men usually self-medicate using vices like drugs, pornography, sex, alcohol, food, and other risky activities. There's a need for them to revisit their pasts so that they can discover the source of their internal pain. Usually, it traces back to a lack of fatherly love and affection and a lack of affirmation from their fathers or a father figure; this left them questioning their value and worth and whether or not they were loved or lovable; this is almost a type of trauma. Perhaps it is. He's stuck in a moment in time where he feels rejected by the most important male figure in his life. That rejection has him living in limbo. He knows you love him, but he can't fully embrace your love because he's still questioning his value and lovability as a man. Most likely, he doesn't feel worthy of your love; he doesn't feel good enough. And this can be tiring and frustrating. But be patient. Things will turn around if you do these:

1. Become a listening ear. One of the things that help all people heal is open communication. Talking about one's problems brings exposure to the hidden things of the heart. The exposure of the hidden thoughts and feelings will usher in the sense of relief through release.
2. Create a judgment-free space. Your man won't open up and share his thoughts and feelings if he

feels like you will judge him because of them. Create an environment where your man feels safe to be vulnerable, realizing he won't be penalized for being honest and open. Let him open up about his emotions while reaffirming him that he still has your respect.
3. Don't invalidate his emotions. Don't make your man feel as if his emotions and issues, regardless of how big or small they may be, aren't serious enough to require your attention. You must communicate to your man that, even if his reality might not seem legit or true, you respect that this is his reality; therefore, it's a big deal not just to him but also to you. Let him know that whatever hurts him hurts you too and that you're in this with him.
4. Encourage him to seek professional help. Counseling should not be seen as a stigma in your home. Sadly, in many communities, counseling is perceived as a service that only caters to people who're mentally insane; however, nothing can be further from the truth. Counseling is for all people, no matter how big or small the trauma or issue. It's always wise to sit down and talk through the things that bother us with people who're specifically trained in dealing with trauma, emotional distress, and psychological issues—which we all experience in life.
5. Remind him of the power of forgiveness. We can't rewind the hands of time and undo the past, but we can free ourselves from the power of the past and even learn and grow from it. But this is only

CHAPTER 2: EVERY MAN NEEDS AFFIRMATION

done through forgiveness. Forgiving others, that father who abandoned him, and that father figure who misled him is necessary for him to release the toxicity he feels that threatens to hold his life hostage and even turn him into the very thing he hates.

EVERY MAN'S LOVE LANGUAGE

In the book *The Five Love Languages*, author Gary Chapman talks about the different ways in which people express their love—and the ways different people want to be loved. One of the love languages listed is *words of affirmation*. For the person with this love language, whenever someone compliments them, encourages them, heaps unexpected praises on them, and verbally expresses how much they mean to them, they feel loved, cherished, and accepted. Many, if not most, men desire words of affirmation from their wives and girlfriends. Boys want to be affirmed by their fathers, and men want to be affirmed by their wives and girlfriends.

It's not a sign of insecurity when a man or woman wants to be told "I love you" by their partner or spouse. According to Chapman, this is a normal desire—a need. We all want and need to hear certain words in our lives. The Bible emphasizes the importance of our words repeatedly. For example, going back to our Scripture from chapter one, Solomon revealed that

"Kind words are like honey—sweet to the soul and healthy for the body." (NLT)

Also, in Proverbs 15:4, the Bible says,

> "Gentle words are a tree of life; a deceitful tongue crushes the spirit." (NLT)

And then there's Proverbs 18:21, which says,

> "Death and life are in the power of the tongue: and they that love it shall eat the fruit thereof." (KJV)

These are a few examples in the Bible. Just a few. The book of James talks about the tongue being the smallest but most powerful and destructive member of our bodies, altering individuals' destinies and entire nations. That means words are more powerful than we know. According to the above Scriptures, words can heal our physical bodies, become a constant source of nourishment for our souls or crush our spirits, and they can bring blessings or curses into our lives (life or death). No wonder Jesus said we'll have to give an account before God during judgment for every idle word we speak (Matthew 12:36).

When you verbally affirm your man, you build him up emotionally and mentally; this gives him the fuel to continue moving forward. On the other hand, when you ignore him or use your tongue to tear him down, this can deplete him and bring a halt to his progress. Men look for environments where they're affirmed, where they're being made to feel accepted and valued. All men want to be assured that they're wanted and needed. All humans prefer to be in environments where they're celebrated as opposed to tolerated. No one wants to stay where they're

CHAPTER 2: EVERY MAN NEEDS AFFIRMATION

not welcomed.

Using your tongue to affirm your man will keep him coming back to you as his source of healing and strength, as we discussed in the previous chapter.

WAYS TO AFFIRM YOUR MAN

As with encouragement, affirmations are positive reinforcement that motivates men to continue with specific behaviors. He may not know if he's doing the right thing by you or doing a good job; therefore, your affirmation lets him know whether or not he's pleasing you and doing the right thing by you. And affirmations apply to every situation, from housework to sex. Let him know by constantly affirming him. Here are a few suggestions:

Write a note affirming him. This is always a good approach, one that has the potential to carry the element of surprise. For example, there's the story of a man whose wife fixed him a packed lunch before sending him off to work. When lunchtime came, he pulled out the ham sandwich she fixed him. When he got ready to bite into it, he noticed a piece of paper sticking out of its side. When he pulled out the paper, he discovered a note from his wife expressing her appreciation for him, telling him how much she loved him. That completely transformed his day and lifted his spirit.

Send him a text. Technology can work in your favor when you use it properly. For example, sending an unexpected text message praising and affirming your man, telling him how proud you are of him and how much you love and appreciate him, will transform his day and work wonders in your relationship. You might even get creative with it and include a pic with the text if you want to spice up the night. Just saying.

Speak words of affirmation. Here are a few words of affirmations to use on him (taken from *103 Words of Affirmation Every Husband Wants to Hear*, from www.faithfulman.com):

- Thanks for being a great husband!
- I'm glad you're my friend.
- You're a great (are going to be a great) Dad!
- Thanks so much for fixing that!
- I really appreciate you.
- When you listened to me, you made me feel loved.
- You are my man!
- You are my protector.
- You are awesome!
- Hey, do you have any plans later?
- I respect you so much.
- Thanks for working so hard.
- You're an excellent provider.
- You make me feel like a Lady.
- I love being with you.
- You're so smart.
- You're amazing!
- Thank you, that was really kind.
- You're so strong.
- When you hold me tight, I feel safe with you.
- Thanks for the date . . . I enjoyed being with you.

CHAPTER 2: EVERY MAN NEEDS AFFIRMATION

- You're a great lover.
- I'll always stand by your side.
- Your secrets are safe with me.
- I'm yours.
- I'll go wherever you lead.
- I'm blessed you are my husband.
- Thank you for leading our family.
- Your ideas are so exciting!
- Thanks for helping around the house.
- It's fun to work with you.
- What a great job – that looks fantastic!
- You are one handsome man.
- I've learned so much from you.
- Our kids are (going to be) fortunate you are their dad.
- I'm a better woman because you're my husband. I mean that.
- You are my favorite person in the entire world!
- I want to grow old with you.
- You're a great kisser.
- I'm thinking we should go to bed early tonight . . .
- I trust your judgment.
- Thank you for caring how I feel.
- I appreciate how you show me respect.
- I have confidence in your leadership.
- I totally trust you.
- You inspire me to be the best I can be.
- You stand for the Truth. I admire that.
- Your enthusiasm get's me excited.
- You're amazing – you really are!
- I wouldn't trade my life with you for anything.

5 THINGS EVERY MAN NEEDS

- I will always be loyal to you.
- No other man could even come close.
- I will always honor you.
- What do you need from me?
- I love being by your side.
- You look great!
- You were amazing last night.
- How can I serve you in a way that makes you feel loved and respected?
- I love it when you teach me (us) the Word of God.
- You have a lot to offer.
- Thank you for being a faithful husband (and father).
- God must really be looking out for me to give me a man like you!
- Being with you is my favorite place to be.
- I hope you slept well last night because I was thinking we'd stay up a little later tonight!
- Our kids really look up to you . . . and so do I.
- I'm grateful our kids have such an excellent role model.
- Do you know how much I love you?
- I'll love you always and forever.

3 | Every Man Needs A Safe Place

ONE OF THE MOST POPULAR STORIES IN the Bible is that of David and King Saul. David was just a child when he met King Saul. His popularity with King Saul developed after he killed a giant named Goliath. This menacing giant struck fear into the hearts of the fighting men of Israel, but not David; he was already used to big opposition, being that he killed a lion and a bear to save his sheep from sudden death. With a slingshot and a smooth rock, David was able to slay the mean, nasty giant and solidify his place in Israelite history, becoming known as a giant-slayer. However, it's what happened after that event that shaped David's life.

After capturing the eye of the king, David became Saul's mentee. He started spending a lot of time with King Saul, serving him faithfully. David was not only a warrior but a poet and skilled musician. He wrote beautiful songs of worship to God. King Saul grew mad with time. According to Scripture, he became tormented by a demonic spirit due to defying God's instructions and losing favor with God; this is where things get interesting. Whenever Saul was being attacked in his mind by the demonic spirit, David would drive the spirit away by playing and singing worship songs to God in Saul's presence. David knew how to bring in the presence and anointing of God into an atmosphere, which brought Saul peace—at least, temporarily.

As time progressed, David's name and reputation grew. He developed into a warrior and became popular with the people; this made Saul jealous. Suddenly, David found himself being hunted down by the very man he regarded as a father figure. Saul went mad and tried to kill David. He made several attempts on David's life. Even in light of the fact that David was his son-in-law, Saul still tried to kill him. Finally, King Saul gathered his entire military and went on the hunt for David. David was now a fugitive on the run, although he hadn't committed a crime; he was blessed and anointed by God, and this made him a target.

When you have the favor of God in your life, not everyone will like you; some people will turn on you and seek to bring you down simply because you're a threat to them. So realize that God's favor brings blessings and persecution.

For nearly a decade, David spent his life on the run from a maniacal mad man. There he was, hiding out in caves, eating what he could when he could, doing everything to avoid being captured and killed. He was es-

CHAPTER 3: EVERY MAN NEEDS A SAFE PLACE

tranged from his family and his wife; he was paranoid, constantly looking over his shoulder; he was alone, afraid, and feeling abandoned. At times, his mind was playing tricks on him. He probably thought God forgot about him and that his life had somehow slipped away. Overnight he went from being a celebrated war hero to being Israel's Most Wanted. He felt like he'd been thrust into the middle of a tornado. He was spinning in a never-ending cycle of fear and shame.

This is typical of life. So many times, we start with such great promise, possessing big dreams and ideas and feeling as if the world is ours for the taking. And then life happens. We end up being thrust into a season of madness and confusion, wondering where our lives went and what happened. The worst part is the shame and guilt we experience during these times. We beat ourselves down as if we did something wrong, dropped the ball, lost opportunities, and even lost favor with God. Of course, none of that is true, but that's how we feel.

And yet, God knows how to comfort us during these seasons in our lives.

God didn't leave David all alone. He sent Jonathan into David's life to be a safe place for him. Yes, Jonathan was Saul's son, but he didn't share his father's obsession and madness. Jonathan was a good man. Although he was a captain in his father's army, he stayed in secret communication with David, helping him avoid capture. He became someone David could confide in, someone David could trust.

David and Jonathan's love for each other was so deep they became covenant brothers. No, they weren't sexually involved; they were committed to each other; this is what the Bible meant by David loved Jonathan more than women (2 Samuel 1:26). Their commitment to each other was more important than anything else in this world. They shared a bond that no one could break, and no one and nothing could come between them.

Let's take a moment and examine what made Jonathan a safe place for David. Jonathan did several things that helped David survive the worst season of his life, things every man needs in his life to remain to be the leader he was created to be and endure the pressures coming against him.

A GOOD LISTENER

Jonathan was a listening ear. Being a good listener isn't natural, at least not for everyone. We must practice good listening skills. These skills will greatly increase our communication with our partners.

People want to be heard. They want to feel like they're understood. Do you know why couples raise their voices and yell during arguments? It's because they feel like they're not being heard and understood. And when they throw out hurtful words, it's because they feel hurt due to not being listened to, and they want their partner to feel their pain; therefore, the goal is to make your partner feel heard and understood during communication.

In an article entitled *What Great Listeners Actually Do*, printed in Harvard Business Review, researchers Jack Zenger and Joseph Folkman identified three main listening practices that characterize effective listening. They are:

CHAPTER 3: EVERY MAN NEEDS A SAFE PLACE

- Not talking when others are speaking
- Letting others know you're listening through facial expressions and verbal sounds ("Mmm-hmm")
- Being able to repeat what others have said, practically word-for-word

Instead of over-talking your partner, give them time to finish their statement. Communication is a challenge for men to begin with, considering how most of them were raised. They already wrestle with opening up and sharing their thoughts and feelings. Most women complain that their men tend to be short in their responses to questions ("How was your day, baby?" "Fine." "Fine? Nothing interesting happened?" "No."). For guys, when their wives or girlfriends ask them detailed questions, they see this as interrogation and automatically become defensive. They weren't taught that open and honest communication is the path to a woman's heart; this is why the art of listening is essential; it helps to facilitate open and honest communication in a relationship, making it easier for a man battling with communication to engage in the process. And it starts with the simple act of respecting your partner when they talk by allowing them to speak without cutting them off.

Whenever you cut your partner off when they're talking, you're communicating to them that their words don't matter to you. For men, when they feel as if their words don't matter in a relationship, they resign to quietness and become absentminded, choosing to opt-out of the entire communication process altogether. A man is not going to attempt to out-talk his woman. He knows he won't win. He knows talking isn't his department to begin with. He'll check out and leave. But when he feels heard, he tends to talk more, he tends to come around more, and he feels more comfortable talking to his partner. She makes him feel like his words are valuable; therefore, she makes him feel valuable and cherished.

If the spark in your relationship has vanished, think about the reason or reasons why. Just think back to the time when you and your partner were in love. If you go back to that place, you'll notice there was one distinct characteristic of your love: you paid close attention to the things your partner said. No one had to teach you this; you instinctively knew that to make your partner feel valuable, you had to show them their words meant the world to you, and you did this by listening intently to every word they said. The two of you could be in a crowded room, but when they spoke, you'd tune everyone and everything out to pay special attention to them. That was your way of communicating your love, respect, and appreciation for them. Unfortunately, with time, that has diminished, and now you probably act as if they have nothing interesting to say. While they're talking, you pull out your cell phone and stroll on your timeline, or you start flipping through the television channels. And now, you're asking, Where has the love gone? It left when you and your partner stopped valuing one another as a priority.

Reignite the spark in your relationship by doing simple things during communication like putting away the gadgets, tuning out or turning off the television, put-

CHAPTER 3: EVERY MAN NEEDS A SAFE PLACE

ting away the books, and teaching the kids to respect boundaries and avoid interrupting when your partner is speaking with you. Instead, please give them your undivided attention. And after they're done making a statement, repeat back to them what they said. Doing this reinforces the fact that you were listening, making them feel even more valued by you. For example:

> **Husband:** I felt like exploding on my boss today. He gets on my nerves. He keeps coming down on my head about every little thing, and yet, he doesn't do that to anyone else on the job.
> **Wife:** So you feel like your boss is singling you out, coming down on your head about every little thing while not doing the same to the other staff? I understand.

The wife summed up her husband's statement, which let him know she was listening. Next, she validated his feelings rather than shun him for how he felt; this will diffuse tension and help him to calm down. Again, by validating his feelings, you're communicating to him that his feelings matter; this is critical for men, being that their first impulse is to dismiss their feelings from the get-go. But little by little, you're helping your man to feel more open about sharing how he feels. By using key phrases like "I understand," "I respect how you feel," "I value your opinion," and "I really appreciate you sharing with me how you feel," you knock the wall of defensiveness down and help to bring your man out. But using phrases like "I can't believe you feel that way" or "That's crazy—you wanted to do what?" will only make your man feel judged and cause them to retreat into their shell, which leads me to my next point.

CREATE A JUDGMENT-FREE ZONE

Jonathan didn't judge David, which made David feel safe opening up to him about his fears and frustrations. Jonathan displayed great empathy.

Mental health experts have identified several characteristics of judgmental people, one of the biggest being a lack of empathy. Empathy is "the ability to understand and share the feelings of others" (dictionary.com). Empathy is your ability to place yourself in another person's shoes and see things through their eyes. This skill makes the difference between a healthy relationship and an unhealthy one. To practice empathy, do what James 1:19 tells us to do:

> "You must all be quick to listen, slow to speak, and slow to get angry" (NLT).

One of the biggest mistakes we make during communication is allowing our emotions to lead us rather than our minds. As a result, we react emotionally rather than process what our partners say intellectually. And I get it—it's hard to keep our feelings in check, especially when we feel like we're being attacked. But when James said we must be quick to listen, he told us to put our emotions aside and carefully analyze what's being said. Often, people's true motives, intentions, and concerns are concealed within their words and nonverbal cues. Listen like a detective

CHAPTER 3: EVERY MAN NEEDS A SAFE PLACE

trying to solve a case, not like a person who wears their heart on their sleeve. And know that what people say isn't always what they mean, so don't take everything personally.

Furthermore, James warns us against overreacting and jumping to conclusions—be slow to speak. Think about what you're going to say before you respond. Consider your words wisely because they can either bring healing or more destruction. Many people have lost their jobs, careers, and reputations because they spoke out of anger and emotion. For example, John H. Schnatter, the founder of Papa John's Pizza, was forced to step down from his position in his company, and he plummeted into public disgrace because he allowed his mouth to get him in trouble. He uttered the "N" word while railing against NFL players during a conference call. I'm sure you can think of plenty of other examples of this.

Proverbs 29:11 says, "A fool uttereth all his mind: but a wise man keepeth it in till afterwards" (KJV). The New Living Translation words it this way:

> "Fools vent their anger, but the wise quietly hold it back."

The worst thing we can do is vent openly while angry. When angry, we don't say the right things. You can deal permanent damage to a marriage or parent/child relationship by talking while angry. You may feel like you've been wronged, but don't exasperate the situation by uttering the wrong words. You'll only add fuel to the fire and make a bad situation worse.

Eliminate judgment by practicing empathy. Doing this will create a safe place for your man and cause him to become less defensive.

FRIENDSHIP

Jonathan was a true friend. Friendship is based on respect and dependability. When we think of a true friend, we picture a person who's willing to sacrifice his or her time for us when needed, someone who genuinely cares about our wellbeing and safety. They'll look out for us and keep our secrets safe while encouraging us to make the right decisions—they don't want to see us destroy ourselves. Proverbs 27:6 says, "Wounds from a sincere friend are better than many kisses from an enemy" (NLT).

Men look for friendship in their partners. They want someone they can confide in and who won't share their secrets. For example, if your man shares a secret with you and you hop on the phone and tell your mom, sister, or best friend, you'll completely shatter his trust in you and destroy the communication between the two of you.

Being what the Bible calls a "talebearer" or "gossip" is not only a bad practice; it's a wicked one. Proverbs 11:13 says, "A gossip betrays confidence, but a trustworthy person keeps a secret" (NIV). Contrary to popular belief, men long to be vulnerable in relationships. They want someplace they can take off their armor and uncover their wounds, but they don't want to suffer the pain of betrayal and humiliation of public embarrassment. In my years of counseling, I've discovered that when there's a breakdown in communication in marriage, it is due to a lack of trust. The husband fears opening up to his wife because he

CHAPTER 3: EVERY MAN NEEDS A SAFE PLACE

fears she'll share his secrets with her mother, sister, or best friend, thereby causing him public shame and humiliation. This fear didn't just show up; it developed as a result of past negative experiences. Perhaps his wife betrayed his trust in the past, and now he struggles with opening up to her. She may not have known the amount of damage she's done by sharing the personal problems in her relationship with her family and friends instead of sharing them with a neutral, third-party professional counselor.

Men longing for friendship in their wives find themselves the most vulnerable and susceptible to outside temptation. Like I stated earlier, affairs aren't based on physical attraction but on emotional connection. Men want to connect emotionally with women to have their need for honor and respect met. Women are especially suited to fulfill these needs in men. When other women pick up on this deficiency in a man, those who lack integrity will hone in on it and prey on the man, luring him away from his marriage and home. She'll present herself as a listening ear and one he can confide in, promising to protect his heart by covering his secrets rather than blasting them out loud; this creates a special bond between them. From there, a deep connection is made, one that often leads to physical intimacy. She's effectively presented herself as his safe place. It doesn't matter that her motives are wrong and her tactics are deceptive; what matters here is that she managed to become what he longs for in a woman. That is how Delilah in the Bible was able to lure Samson into her bosom and cause him to rest his head in her lap. She reduced the strongest, most powerful man on the planet to nothing, not by using looks (and don't get me wrong, looks certainly play a role, just not the biggest role), but by winning his trust by presenting herself as a true friend. Listening to him. Not judging him. Being available to him. Paying him special attention. Showing him the utmost respect. Honoring him. Creating an atmosphere where he felt safe being vulnerable. Picture the mighty Samson, after killing over a thousand Philistines with his bare hands and after ripping the jaw off of an adult male lion, walking into Delilah's tent and laying his head on her bosom and weeping like a baby. He'd tell her about his hurts and pains, fears and frustrations, reveal the sadness in his heart and reveal to her the little boy hiding behind his tough exterior. She was able to unmask the little boy within through the power of seduction. Sadly, he paid for it in the end. But think about the damage that could have been prevented if he'd found a safe place in the right woman. Are you being a safe place for your man or creating an environment in the home that makes him look for a safe place outside of the home?

TRUST

Without trust, you have no relationship. When communication and fun disappear in a relationship, chances are there's a lack of trust. I hear this a lot: "My husband comes from a family where they don't speak. Everyone is quiet. That's why he won't talk to me." Trust me when I say your husband's upbringing doesn't matter; communication, affection, and intimacy are basic needs every person has. Your husband wants to share his heart with you, but he may feel like he cannot trust you.

Trust in relationships is destroyed by three key

CHAPTER 3: EVERY MAN NEEDS A SAFE PLACE

things: a lack of transparency, damaging words, and disrespect.

If you're not transparent with your partner, they won't trust you. They'll assume you're up to no good and holding secrets from them. Opening up secret bank accounts, creating fake social media profiles and reaching out to old flames, and living a double life will shatter the trust in your relationship. Such activities will leave your partner feeling like you're planning a life without him and are waiting for the perfect moment to make your exit. In preparation for what they believe is the inevitable betrayal, your partner will immediately move to protect their heart, perceiving you as a potential threat. And you'll notice their change in attitude towards you—how they're suddenly acting very guarded around you.

Damaging words can obliterate trust. Many times couples will say hurtful things, not thinking about the long-term consequences of their words. Even after forgiving and making up, the sting is still there, and a slight hesitation lingers in the air. Your partner feels reluctant to fully engage with you, fearing they will get pounded on again if they make a mistake.

No one is entitled to use their tongue destructively simply because they're irritated or vexed. When you're loose in the tongue, speaking out of emotions rather than out of wisdom, you will be perceived as unstable. And if there's one characteristic that exemplifies the opposite of safety, it's instability.

You are not a safe place if you can't control your tongue and temper your words. In your relationship, you'll be perceived as a minefield, and your partner will soon grow weary of tip-toeing when around you. That's mentally exhausting.

Every man wants peace. Men don't handle emotional pressure as easily as women, who are a lot tougher in that department. Biologically, men are hardwired differently than women and can't function as smoothly when their blood pressure surpasses a certain point. That's why most men walk away during a heated argument. When this happens too often, that household will represent tension and toxic emotion to him and resemble a battlefield rather than a safe place. He will be more anxious to leave than stay and will begin staying out later and later. He will prefer to stay at work, at the sports bar or another woman's house. Again, he wants a place where he can unwind, not be wound up.

Proverbs 21:9 says, "Better to live on a corner of the roof than share a house with a quarrelsome wife" (NIV). The word *quarrelsome* in the Hebrew language is translated as "contentious, brawling." The word *contentious* is defined as "causing or likely to cause an argument" (www.dictionary.com). Notice here it is the woman who sets the tone in the home and not the man. She creates a pleasant or unpleasant atmosphere, and she does it with her tongue. A contentious or brawling woman loves to wind her man up by using trigger words she knows will start an argument. She doesn't practice prudence and wisdom, carefully planning the right time to address certain things. She doesn't consider the tone of her voice and method of approach when bringing up certain issues. She instead lets her tongue rip and then justifies her destructive words by claiming she's emotional or it's simply the way she is—it's

CHAPTER 3: EVERY MAN NEEDS A SAFE PLACE

her personality. Foolishness is not a personality trait; it's the byproduct of a lack of godly wisdom.

Men run from brawling, argumentative, belligerent wives who enjoy turning their homes into battlefields, and they're drawn to women who practice "the unfading beauty of a gentle and quiet spirit, which is so precious to God" (1 Peter 3:4, NLT). Her calm demeanor calms him down, which is where he needs to be if he's going to communicate. Her gentleness, tone and approach relaxes him, which makes him feel safe. Peter even said this type of spirit not only transforms the atmosphere in the home, making it comfortable for the husband, but it pleases God. He said it melts the hearts of even the hardest men.

Another thing that destroys trust is disrespect. *Respect* is defined as "due regard for the feelings, wishes, rights, or traditions of others" (www.dictionary.com). Now we all have little quirks and habits that irritate our partners, but out of respect, we should be considerate of how these things affect our partners. Consideration is the key. If what you're doing irks your partner in a major way, then what hurts them should concern you. The two of you should feel comfortable enough to share these things and be willing to come to a compromise. But when you take the attitude that "this is nonnegotiable," then you shut down communication and communicate a lack of respect or consideration for your partner.

Respect is a need of all people, but it's a mega need of men. Many women I've counseled were oblivious of the many ways they communicated disrespect to their husbands. Some hadn't even realized how much they had lost respect for their husbands. Because of this, I feel compelled to remind you that love and respect are not conditional. According to the Bible, these things must be unconditional. In other words, a husband is instructed in Ephesians 5:25 to love his wife the way Christ loves the church, which means to love her without conditions attached. He's not to love his wife if she treats him fairly or does what he wants her to do; he's to love her regardless, which means to put her needs first and to esteem her highly, making her his priority. Likewise, in verse 22 of that chapter, Paul instructs wives to "submit to your own husbands, as unto the Lord." By submit, he means to respect him as the head of the household and defer to his leadership. Yes, the husband and the wife are to work together, but there can only be one head like any team or organization. When you have two visions for a company or organization, you have di-vision (the prefix "di" means "double; twice"). Division is having two different visions. God called the man to be the visionary for the family and the wife to be his helper; He didn't commission the wife to operate in her own vision at the expense of ripping off the head. Paul said she must submit to the vision of her husband. But again, this may be difficult, especially when she has a man who doesn't seem to have a vision or whose vision seems off. However, she's forgetting or underestimating the meaning of "helping." She's not called to wonder helplessly; she's there to help steer him in the right direction. As the saying goes, the man may be the head, but the wife is the neck, and the neck controls the head. However, there's a subtle line here. As a wife, she's called to be a godly influence over her husband, not control him. She's not supposed to act in place of God in his

CHAPTER 3: EVERY MAN NEEDS A SAFE PLACE

life but to pray earnestly for him and remind him to seek God for the vision for the home. She attempts to control him when she uses manipulation, criticism, bad words, and nagging to get him to do what she wants him to do. She is not helping him at that point; she is disrespecting him.

Belittling your partner to motivate them is wrong. Belittling them doesn't motivate them; it discourages them. Furthermore, criticizing your partner doesn't cause them to discontinue certain habits; it only drives them further away from you. Like we discussed in the first chapter, criticism keeps the focus on what your partner isn't doing rather than highlighting what they're doing right. The way to motivate people is to remind them of their ability and praise their successes, not remind them of their shortcomings and shame them for having them. Heaping praises on your man and building his ego won't lead him astray; it will simply cause him to turn his heart towards you and value what you have to say more. And it's at that moment that you have the opportunity to influence his decisions.

Peter and Paul reveal to godly wives that by submitting to and honoring their husbands, they're doing something in the spirit realm that will benefit them tremendously: they are demonstrating faith in God. Peter said her reverence for her husband is pleasing to God, and Paul said her submission to her husband is being done "unto the Lord." God is watching how she deals with her husband, and based on this, determines how He deals with her. God loves us all, but He's no respecter of person. When we honor Him by doing that which pleases Him,

He then moves on our behalf and blesses us; this applies even when we do that which is right towards those who mistreat us. God will bless us for our obedience and punish them for their disobedience. The wife who submits to her husband's leadership and honors him as the head, reverencing him and building him up, has the biggest weapon of all on her side: a God who'll fight for her. Her prayers carry more weight because of her respectful behavior towards her husband. When she intercedes for her husband, he can't help but hear and feel God moving him in another direction. When he mistreats her, he won't be able to rest comfortably at night; He'll have no peace. He'll either straighten up and get with the program or God will move him out of the picture entirely. But make no doubt about it, God is in control, not her. She's simply pleasing God by honoring her husband, and God is honoring her prayer to transform and guide her husband. God is doing what only He can in the situation while she does her part.

The Bible doesn't say respect your husband if he acts in a manner pleasing to you. He doesn't have to be what you want him to be for you to respect him. He doesn't have to act "worthy and deserving" of your respect, but rather, you should respect your husband because this causes the favor of God to flow in your life. Your respectful and reverent attitude towards your husband moves the hand of the only One that can change a person's heart and change their life.

Since respect is the key issue here, let's look at a few other ways wives disrespect their husbands, often without knowing it. First, disrespecting your husband's parenting style and authority as a parent shows your lack

CHAPTER 3: EVERY MAN NEEDS A SAFE PLACE

of respect for him. Furthermore, questioning his authority in front of the kids is a big no-no. When a man's wife challenges his parental authority, he'll usually shut down and become less involved in the parenting responsibility, leaving the wife to bear the burden alone. That will cause him to feel ashamed and become withdrawn, and it will have a negative impact on the kids.

As a wife and mother, if you're in a blended family, you must teach your children to respect your man, even though he's not the biological father. Training your children to respect authority is your responsibility. They have to learn how to respect teachers they may not like, coaches, and eventually their bosses. So why is it any different to teach them to respect a man in the home who's not the biological father? They don't have to call him dad, but they do have to respect him. And as a stepdad, he shouldn't be left to bear the burden of gaining respect alone; his wife—their mother—should be the enforcer, getting on them about their disrespectful attitudes and putting her foot down. And vice-versa. As a husband and father, he must train his children to respect his wife.

Another way wives disrespect their husbands is by treating them like they're one of the kids—essentially, acting like you are your man's mother. You can avoid this temptation by bringing up concerns or grievances with your husband in that soft tone we discussed earlier and without the presence of the children. The worst example parents can give to children is to openly correct and work out problems in front of the children.

Another way wives disrespect their husbands is by embarrassing them in public. Wives embarrass their husbands by talking about their shortcomings and the problems in their relationships with family members and friends. Wives also disrespect their husbands by correcting them publicly in front of others, yelling at them in public, flirting with other men in front of them, and interrupting and silencing them when they are speaking publicly. For most men, being humiliated in public is a death blow to their egos. Doing this can build resentment in your man's heart towards you. That resentment will show up in many ways; the first is the shutdown of communication, the second being an emotional withdrawal from the relationship. From there, things only tend to get worse. If there's something you need to say to your husband, pick the right time to address it. If you have to whisper in his ear, send him a text, or pull him aside politely, that is a lot better than correcting or criticizing him in front of people. But remember always to build up his public image, not tear it down.

Lastly, another way wives disrespect their husbands is by depriving them of sex, which leads me to my next chapter—

4 | Every Man Needs Sex

I WANT YOU TO PICTURE THIS SCENARIO: a woman finds herself asking her husband, "What's wrong, honey?"

"Nothing," he mutters briefly. His face, however, betrays his words, revealing the fact that something is bothering him. Not only is his countenance revealing this, but his nonverbal behavior is also. He's acting cold and distant. That gentle, warm attitude he normally displays has vanished. He's less talkative; short in his responses to her questions. He seems indifferent towards her. He doesn't have to admit it, but she recognizes resentment when she sees it; the hallmark signs are present and glaring.

Of course, she has a lot on her mind as well. The kids. Perhaps her job is weighing on her mind. Maybe some bills need to be paid. She feels stressed, overextended and alone in handling household duties, balancing her domestic life, social life, and professional life like so many other women. She's thinking that the faucet is still dripping, among other household tasks she needs help with. So, naturally, she looks to her husband for support. He'd normally do things around the house without having to be asked. He'd help in every way possible, knowing this pleases her. But now, he's acting unloving and uncaring.

What the wife doesn't see is the build-up of sexual tension inside her husband, accompanied by a sense of shame and embarrassment over having to ask for sex. He wonders why he has to ask or even beg for something that he was promised while at the altar. In his mind, he signed up for a lifetime supply of something he needs only to be repeatedly denied it by the only person qualified to give it to him.

Battling through feelings of embarrassment, humiliation, and resentment, he juggles his loyalty to his marriage and his desire for sexual fulfillment. Then finally, after enough cold showers and long nights at the gym, he eventually confronts her about his need. He tells her he is upset over the lack of intimacy and informs her that something has to change; or worse, he doesn't confront her but instead chooses to have his needs met outside the marriage. As a result, he turns to pornography and adulterous affairs. That's when things get ugly.

All too often, we've seen this scenario play out. It usually occurs when people take one another for granted and ignore each other's needs. One person stops prioritizing his or her partner's needs over other things and unknowingly begins to devalue their partner. You don't

CHAPTER 4: EVERY MAN NEEDS A SEX

have to use negative and harsh words to tear down and devalue your partner; all you have to do is ignore their basic needs. And many couples doom their relationships from the very beginning by not educating themselves on their partner's needs.

For men, sex is one of their biggest needs next to respect and honor. Sex is how men connect with their wives and form stronger bonds of intimacy with them. In the same way that women need security and open communication, men need sex. They are hardwired that way. Their desire for sex isn't based on selfishness but biology. For example, men produce 1,500 sperm per second, which means they constantly crave sexual release. I'm not suggesting men are purely driven by sex, but sex is a major factor in their lives, one that influences their decision-making more than anything when it comes to choosing a partner.

THE CONFUSION OVER SEX

Although sex is one of the biggest needs of men in marriage, truthfully speaking, it is a major part of everyone's life, whether you believe it or not. If not for sex, none of us would be here. But while sex is a huge part of the human experience and an intricate part of our lives, the subject is deeply shrouded and taboo in many circles, especially in many churches. Because of this, there's a lot of confusion about sex.

If you were to listen to the entertainment industry, they'd have you believing sex is a rite of passage into social acceptance. The secular media shames and ridicules those who view sex as sacred. Such was the case with Sean

Lowe of The Bachelor, a popular television show where ladies compete for the attention of a male suitor. Sean and his top pick on the show, Catherine Giudici, who later became his wife, decided to wait until marriage before having sex. The media criticized them relentlessly for their decision, depicting them as odd and out of touch with reality.

You can barely turn on the television and not be inundated by a flood of sexual references, images, and propaganda. Sex and violence are at the core of seemingly every Hollywood film and television show. They aim to popularize premarital and non-traditional sex. And we don't want to talk about the porn industry—it glorifies sexual violence and unrealistic sexual situations that give people unrealistic expectations.

Not only is Hollywood screwed up when it comes to sex, but the music industry also. Much of today's music is filled with sexually degrading lyrics that objectify women. Even female artists tend to objectify women in their songs to increase sales.

With the entertainment industry as their guide, young people today have discounted the sanctity and sacredness of sex and its importance. For this reason, we see a generation of selfish, self-centered, narcissistic people who struggle with building and maintaining satisfying and lasting relationships.

Equally as damaging are the distortions about sex many of us receive from our family and friends. For example, you may have received advice about men and women from a promiscuous friend. They have a long history of bad relationships where sex was misused, and they began

CHAPTER 4: EVERY MAN NEEDS A SEX

to spill their poison into your ears, teaching you how to do the same. Your friend thinks monogamy is being with one man at a time, and she's with a different man every other week or every other night. She tells you that men only want one thing and feeds you the idea that sex is about power and control rather than intimacy and connection. For the guy, he was taught by an older sibling or relative how to be a playa' and lie to get between a girl's legs. His mentors may have told him that his manhood is predicated on how many women he sleeps with. He may have been shown a picture of Wilt Chamberlain as the glaring image of masculinity. To him, sex is a tool of conquest used to give him an inflated sense of importance. Both are wrong.

And then there's the religious distortion concerning sex. Some people have come out of strict religious households where sex was seen as filthy and dirty, even sinful. They heard negative messages about sex while in church, being told that the only people who liked sex in the Bible were prostitutes and courtesans like Delilah. And you don't want to be a Delilah, do you?

Furthermore, it's not always what we are told that shapes our view of sex, but what we were shown. For example, you may have seen your mother bring home man after man each night or your father come home night after night with another woman's lipstick on his shirt collar. Chances are, this has painted a picture of sex in your mind as anything but sacred. Or worse, you may have been the victim of sexual abuse and now abhor sex or view it as a bargaining tool in the relationship.

In any case, we are facing a phenomenon of either

hyper-sexualized or under-sexualized people. Sex is either blown out of proportion or not given the priority status it deserves. Our marriages are suffering due to these distortions and lies about sex, and broken marriages lead to broken communities and a broken society as a whole. We are quite literally in a crisis due to society's misunderstanding of sex.

But rather than turning to mom and dad, your girlfriends or homeboys, the experts, therapists, teachers, relatives, and other people, why not turn to the Creator of sex Himself: God. He made it. He should know more than any of us its intent and purpose. So what does He have to say about sex? (And I can assure you, He has much to say about it.)

A DIVINE PERSPECTIVE

God doesn't hide the truth about sex. He makes it abundantly clear regarding its importance and necessity in marriage. In 1 Corinthians chapter seven, He addresses the topic. There, the Apostle Paul wrote,

> "Now for the matters you wrote about: 'It is good for a man not to have sexual relations with a woman.' But since sexual immorality is occurring, each man should have sexual relations with his own wife, and each woman with her own husband. The husband should fulfill his marital duty to his wife, and likewise the wife to her husband. The wife does not have authority over her own body but yields it to her husband. In the same way, the husband does not have authority over his own body but yields

CHAPTER 4: EVERY MAN NEEDS A SEX

it to his wife. Do not deprive each other except perhaps by mutual consent and for a time, so that you may devote yourselves to prayer. Then come together again so that Satan will not tempt you because of your lack of self-control." (vs. 1-5, NIV)

Those were powerful words about the importance of sex in marriage. Paul said sex is for the marriage union only; it is a fruit designed to be enjoyed by married couples, not singles. To resolve sexual longing or burning passion, Paul prescribed marriage; this reveals that sex is the biggest factor in marriage; it's what makes marriage different from all other relationships in our lives. In other words, we marry not for friendship or business or spiritual growth; we marry for sex and procreation.

Paul said sex is so important in a marriage that couples must have it constantly "so that Satan will not tempt you because of your lack of self-control." In other words, a healthy sex life in marriage will keep the devil out of your home. Notice Paul didn't say a healthy prayer life or a robust bank account will keep Satan out; he said good sex would. Why? What's so special about sex? It's because sex fulfills both physical and emotional needs, and when our needs are met, we become less vulnerable and desperate. Negative emotions such as anger and resentment will melt away when our needs are met. We'll be less likely to exaggerate our partner's flaws and ignore their positive qualities when we feel they are prioritizing our needs.

Emotions are important. We can't simply dismiss them from our lives, nor undermine the connection they have to the spirit world. Paul cautioned us in Ephesians 4:26-27, "Be angry, and yet do not sin; do not let the sun go down on your anger, and do not give the devil an opportunity" (NASB). When we harbor sour emotions, we usually open the door for sin to enter our lives. We entertain sinful thoughts and desires when angry and upset. So the way we shut the door in sin's face is to minimize its opportunity to influence us due to unmet needs.

When the wife withholds sex from her husband, this leads to him feeling rejected and undesired. Rejection is dangerous because it causes us to question ourselves and our worth. It makes us wonder whether or not we're adequate, lovable, and deserving of respect. All of this is going through a husband's mind when his wife repeatedly refuses his sexual advances. She thinks she's simply refusing the act of sex, but in his mind, she's rejecting him as a man. In his world, sex is inextricably tied to his self-esteem as a man. When his wife flirts with him and initiates sex, this makes him feel desirable. When he feels wanted, his self-esteem rises. He feels needed and important. He feels loved and lovable.

WHAT THOTS CAN TEACH WIVES

A few years ago, Lifetime Movie Network produced a movie entitled *The Client List* starring Jennifer Love-Hewitt. The film was based on actual events. It told the story of a young wife and mother who was struggling to make ends meet. Her husband was a hard worker, but he wasn't bringing home enough money through his job. The young woman (Riley) then sought work at a massage parlor that turned out to be a front for a prostitution ring.

CHAPTER 4: EVERY MAN NEEDS A SEX

Top individuals would show up (politicians, judges, pillars of the community, even pastors) to be serviced by the beautiful young women. During her time there, Riley learned what made men tick. After all, if she couldn't turn on her customers, she missed out on their money. But the most important skill she learned that made her the parlor's top attraction was the ability to make her clients feel desired. She'd talk to each of them like they were the sexiest and most attractive things on the planet. She'd build them up with her words. She'd find out what their fantasies were and play the part. In some cases, she'd simply become a listening ear, allowing them to vent without feeling judged. She discovered that if she made her clients feel like a million bucks, they'd pay her a million bucks—they'd bend over backwards for her.

Men love to be built up. They love to be made to feel wanted and needed, and there's no better way to do this than to not only welcome your man's sexual advances but to initiate sex. Flirt with him throughout the day. Tell him he has something special waiting for him at the house once he gets off of work. Put on that sexy dress, those heels, that sexy outfit and cause him to develop whiplash from turning his head so fast just to get a glimpse of you.

Riley learned what the Bible has been declaring for ages: men are visual and love to be seduced. Job 31:1 says, "I made a covenant with my eyes not to look with lust at a young woman" (NLT). Here, Job remarks upon the struggle every man has, which is to control his eyes around attractive women. He's primarily snared by what he sees, which is why his wife has the important job of satisfying his eyes at home. Visual stimulation is one of his biggest needs. That's why most husbands tend to buy sexy clothes for their wives—they are seeking to satisfy their need for such stimulation. Furthermore, men have to fight to tune out all of the visual stimulation being sent their way in the streets, television, the internet, at work, and more. Your husband chose you, not some other woman. He wants to see your body, not another woman's body. He wants to gaze upon your beauty and "drink from his own well" (Proverbs 5:15); however, if you decide not to meet his need for visual stimulation, then you only increase the likelihood that he will turn elsewhere to meet that need. And by this, I mean other women and porn. You help to open the door to sin in his life because you don't know he needs visual stimulation or simply don't care to meet it.

Proverbs 6:24 describes the seductress as having the "smooth tongue of a promiscuous woman" (NLT). Proverbs 2:16 says this woman "flatters with her words" (NKJV). Not only does she dress provocatively, but she likes to flirt. She flirts by building up the man. She brags on him, making him feel like he's the best thing since sliced bread. She praises his accomplishments and avoids criticizing his failures and shortcomings. She makes him believe he can do anything. She knows that if she builds him up with her tongue, he'll become more vulnerable with her. She knows how to make a man fall in love with her. For her, it is simple: appeal to his eyes and his ears. Look sexy and build him up with praise.

Sadly, many women will do these things to get the man and then discontinue them after getting married. That's why Riley was so successful. Her client list didn't consist of single men looking for a good time, but it mainly consisted of married men whose wives had stopped working to attract them and had grown comfortable and settled.

Your man might not cheat on you like the men in the movie did to their wives, but that doesn't make things any less painful. The communication in your relationship may suffer because of his unmet needs. Resentment may drive a rift between the two of you because of his unmet needs. The children may suffer because of his unmet needs—having to grow up in a household filled with arguing and bickering, and disunity. Your needs may go unmet due to his needs not being met. You may begin to feel like you're trapped, married to a brick, all because you failed to meet these needs. Now you're miserable.

Jesus gave us the remedy for relationships that have gone stale. He said in Revelation 2:4-5,

> "But I have this against you, that you have left your first love. 'Therefore remember from where you have fallen, and repent and do the deeds you did at first" (NASB)

He was speaking to the love of His life, the church, and telling them that our relationship with Him had grown stale. We fell out of love with Him. We abandoned our "first love," and now it was time to come back to Him. But how? How can Believers rekindle the fire in their hearts for God? How can they reignite the flame in their relationship with God? Simple. Jesus said we must "do the deeds you did at first."

Do what you did to make your man first notice

you and fall in love with you. If you go back and revisit the things you did first to get his attention and make him fall for you, you will notice that you paid special attention to your appearance and were extra cautious with your words around him. You dressed sexy when he was around, and you heaped praises on him constantly. And you enjoyed the results of your actions: the undivided attention that he showed you, the way he pursued you, the sacrifices he made to show you he loved you and cared about you. As a woman, you have the power to turn him on or turn him off. If the spark is missing in your marriage, take a moment to examine your current actions. Compare your actions to the things you used to do at the beginning of the relationship. Ask yourself if you've changed or have grown lazy and settled. Marriage is work. If you don't put in the work, you won't reap the benefits. If you let your marriage lie idle, it will grow old and rust. It won't fix itself.

WHAT ELSE DID GOD SAY?

In Hebrews 13:4, God says, "Marriage is honourable in all, and the bed undefiled" (KJV). In context, when the writer says the marriage bed is undefiled, this means sex in marriage is pure and must remain pure. Outside of marriage, sex is impure. Also, when we introduce outsiders into our marriage beds, we defile the marriage beds. Therefore, we must keep sex sacred. However, what this is not addressing is sexual positions and experimental activities during sex. Let me make it plain for you: this verse says nothing about oral sex, sex toys, or any other sexual activity that's enjoyed by a couple. The only thing it prohibits is intro-

CHAPTER 4: EVERY MAN NEEDS A SEX

ducing third parties into the bedroom, including pornography (remember Jesus warned us against lusting after another person in our hearts in Matthew 5:27-28). I know you probably heard preachers talk about different sexual activities and regard them as sinful; however, they tend not to have any scriptural basis for their claims. Most of what you hear are opinions, not biblical exegesis. In reality, God wants you and your partner to enjoy each other to the fullest. The only rule is the two of you must flow together in mutual agreement and consent. Sex is meant for your pleasure.

A DEEPER CONNECTION

Men crave sex to connect with their wives; this connection fulfills a deep emotional need in men. In his article *Male Sexuality and Emotional Needs*, Marc DiJulio, MD of Innovative Men's Clinic in Lynnwood, WA, wrote,

> "What drives a man's sexual desire is feeling connected, wanting to be close to his partner - and not just in a physical way. The emotion is: 'I want to experience her. I want to be close. I want to feel love.' I've heard men say that they've felt desire when they sat on the couch and rubbed their partner's feet, shared a bottle of wine, or went camping. There was a shared experience. Deep communication came up as well. Men said they felt desire when they felt heard by their partner when they were on the same page. They would say things like: 'I really felt that my partner saw me, that she got me at that moment.'" (InnovativeMen.com)

It may sound strange to some women, but men are always craving intimate connection with their partners. Always! That's the true driving force behind male sexuality. He wants to please and feel a deep sense of closeness with his wife. It's interesting that when the Bible describes the act of sex, it uses the word "know" or "knew" (Genesis 4:1 says, "And Adam knew Eve his wife; and she conceived"). Sex establishes the deep emotional and even spiritual connection a man desires to have with his partner. And yes, I said spiritual. "How can sex establish a spiritual connection between a man and a woman?" you ask. The Apostle Paul wrote in 1 Corinthians 6:15-16,

> "Don't you realize that your bodies are actually parts of Christ? Should a man take his body, which is part of Christ, and join it to a prostitute? Never! And don't you realize that if a man joins himself to a prostitute, he becomes one body with her? For the Scriptures say, 'The two are united into one.'" (NLT)

Think about that. When the Bible describes two people having sex, it says they are becoming "one". That is where the idea of soul-ties originates. So likewise, people who're sexually involved become one body and soul. They're bonding on the deepest level; this transcends the physical. Trust me. Your man notices the changes in your physical body over time, and yet, he still wants to bond with you. Why? It's because sex is an expression of his longing-ness and desire for you; it is his expression of love and deep

CHAPTER 4: EVERY MAN NEEDS A SEX

passion for you. He wants to show you how he feels about you in his heart through sex. It's how he communicates what he's feeling towards you. That is why sex gets better with age and time in a functional relationship. The more experiences a couple creates and shares, the greater their appreciation for one another. This appreciation fuels the sexual passion they have for each other.

Men need to bond; they require connection to feel valued and needed. There is a danger in bonding with the wrong type of woman, of course. This point is mainly for men. You must bond with a woman of substance, not a "container" (a woman lacking substance, character, and wisdom). Many men have sought to connect with women that were not ready for marriage, and after giving their hearts away to these women, they ended up crushed and devastated, even suicidal. That highlights why God tells us to wait until marriage for sex. Before giving your body and soul away to someone, make sure they're worth the risk. You will want to ensure that you're finding "a wife," not just a woman. Take note from King Solomon, the man who had one-thousand wives. He eventually went crazy because he tried to please all of these women; this led him down a dark path where he turned his back on God and nearly lost everything. The Bible talks about a "virtuous woman" in Proverbs 31, and it tells us that "The man who finds a wife finds a treasure, and he receives favor from the LORD" (Proverbs 18:22, NLT). A wife is a rare breed—a woman who possesses the wisdom and grace to stand alongside a godly man and help him build his vision.

5 THINGS EVERY MAN NEEDS

OH, IT'S GOOD FOR YOU, TOO

We've covered the deeper benefits of sex for men, but let me take just a second and share with you one last pointer about sex. Sex is good not just for the man, but for women, too. For example, here is a list of sexual benefits compiled from books and articles written by medical experts. Sex...

- strengthens your immune system
- lowers your blood pressure
- lowers risks of heart attacks
- is a form of exercise
- decreases physical pain in the body
- decreases the chance of prostate cancer
- improves sleep
- alleviates stress
- decreases depression and anxiety
- makes you look and feel younger
- and increases libido
- sex boosts self-esteem
- makes you feel whole
- increases intimacy
- even makes you smarter

I know that sounds strange. That is, having sex can increase your immune system and help you fight off colds, the flu, and other illnesses that would try to attack your body. Who'd ever thought of sex in that way?—as a form of medicine, as a relaxing agent that soothes the body and melts away stress, as a psychotropic drug that can fight off depression and anxiety. For a moment, go back to my

CHAPTER 4: EVERY MAN NEEDS A SEX

opening example of a sexless marriage. The husband's need for sex is going unfulfilled; this is aiding the mounting tension, stress, and anxiety riding his shoulders, not to mention the depression that typically follows these feelings. And day by day, this stress and anxiety build. Sure, a conversation would be nice. I'm sure he'd enjoy talking about his feelings. But what would relieve and relax him enough to loosen up and engage in a hearty conversation would be a nice dose of sex. In essence, it takes the edge off, allowing him to be in a better position to do the other things.

For women, they tend to take longer to get warmed up for sex. They require a lot of romancing and communication. The old saying is women are like crockpots while men are like microwaves when it comes to sex. However, as we all know, there are moments when it's too tedious to wait for a meal. You need to quickly pop something in the microwave or go by McDonald's or Burger King to satisfy your intense hunger. You don't have the time to wait for a Filet Mignon to cook. Well, the same is true regarding sex. Sometimes you have to have a "quickie" and then save the specially prepared meal for later. The quickie not only tells your man you love him and value his needs, but it also recharges your battery so that you can go on a little further. You need it, too.

You might not feel like doing it at first, but once you start, you'll be glad you did. You will remind your body why sex is so vital as you experience a flood of euphoria, calm and relaxation, and physical and emotional closeness with your partner. You'll feel better, just like him.

5 THINGS EVERY MAN NEEDS

5 | Every Man Needs Accountability

THERE'S A FAMOUS VERSE IN THE BIBLE that highlights the importance of having other people in our lives that can hold us accountable in life. Proverbs 27:17 says, "As iron sharpens iron, so one person sharpens another" (NIV). That verse implicitly states that we cannot sharpen ourselves; we need others to do that. It used to be commonly known that no one can succeed on their own nor survive on their own. People once had a working understanding of how the world truly works—that all of us depend on each other.

There's also that old African proverb that says, "It takes a village to raise a child." The older generations relied heavily on a community; they talked and looked out for each other. They sat around the dinner table and talked, getting to know one another. Some of us grew up in communities where everyone knew each other and where teachers, neighbors, and church mothers were just as involved in disciplining us as our parents. We were taught to respect our elders.

Nowadays, people are strangers living under a single roof. That sense of family is gone. Instead, the kids are all floating in virtual worlds—their heads bowed, and eyes transfixed on their smartphone screens. They hardly look up, and they barely talk. They rarely interact with one another outside of texting. And the parents are no different.

In recent years, a rash of divorces has been attributed to a new addiction: cell phone addiction. One partner is lying in bed wanting attention from the other who's become lost in a digital world, oblivious to their partner. Neglect sets in, and then resentment builds. Next, there's the silent treatment, angry outbursts and yelling, arguing and bickering, all of which leads the relationship down an even darker path.

People have become too distracted to focus on each other. It's too easy to be distracted these days. We carry distractions around in the palms of our hands daily, constantly looking down at them. The ping they let out occasionally steals our attention, pulling us away from whatever task is at hand. We rarely ever take a break from the continual flood of news, gossip and information being pumped into our brains; this comes at a great cost—for, in the end, it is our relationships that suffer the most.

WHY YOU'RE TOGETHER

A relationship will not grow itself, nor will it manage itself no more than a car will change its oil, or a house

CHAPTER 5: EVERY MAN NEEDS ACCOUNTABILITY

will perform its repairs. A relationship can only survive if the couple is mentally present, emotionally available, and committed to maintaining it. That requires us to lay aside the distractions and tend to our partner's needs. We must make them a priority. We must make growing the relationship a priority, and the best way to do this is to help one another grow and develop personally.

The real reason why you and your partner are together is to help each other grow and develop. The relationship shouldn't be centered around business, ministry, or even the kids. The kids will grow up one day and move on with their lives, leaving you and your partner all alone again. What then will you be left with after the kids are gone? That's why it's dangerous to get so tied up with the kids that you ignore your relationship with your partner. That's also the main reason why so many couples divorce after the kids move out. Both parties slowly turned into strangers that co-parent rather than friends and lovers who continually invested time into each other.

You must keep your relationship front and center, and be willing to embark upon the journey of personal development and healing together, holding each other accountable to the process. You must be prepared to deepen the intimacy between the two of you by unmasking and exposing the hidden wounds and scars concealed in your hearts. This kind of unmasking can only take place in a safe, judgment-free environment. You must make your commitment known upfront, letting your partner know that whatever they share with you about him or herself, you won't judge them for it; instead, you only seek to understand them better so that you can serve them better.

Again, this goes back to our earlier chapter, where we discussed the importance of being a good listener. Carve out a distraction-free zone where you put away all of the gadgets and devices and take time to dive into each other's secret worlds.

Get ready to show them your scars, flaws, fears and tears.

When you and your partner first met, you were careful not to reveal any of your flaws and shortcomings. You wore masks and put your best foot forward. You were afraid that if your partner saw the real you, the deeply flawed you, they'd run for the hills. Ironically, they were thinking the same thing—that if you saw the real them, you'd run for the hills. So both of you hid things about yourselves from each other, at least in the beginning. However, over time, those masks began to come down, and those hidden flaws started to come to the surface of the relationship. You began to notice the temper, the bad habits, harmful coping methods, the triggers that cause outbursts and passive-aggressive behavior, and more. At times, you find yourself searching for the initial reason you fell in love with your partner beneath the shuffle of negative emotions. In reality, this reveals a fatal flaw in our thinking:

We believe we shouldn't have to deal with someone else's baggage and that our spouse should come whole and lacking nothing. We think we should be complete before becoming one with another, but that's not true. No one is entirely put together. We're all broken people. We all have a past we are not proud of, have made mistakes we wish we could erase, and deal with shortcomings, temp-

CHAPTER 5: EVERY MAN NEEDS ACCOUNTABILITY

tations, sins and iniquities—all of us. And I hate to be the bearer of bad news, but we're going to have to live with these things until the day that we die. This world is in a fallen state, and we have a fallen, sinful nature to wrestle with daily. So the person you hook up with will come with flaws, plenty of them. They're going to come with plenty of issues. If you think about it, when you receive a spouse, you're receiving the product of generations of dysfunction, abuse, bad habits, wrong thinking, sins and iniquities. You're hooking up with someone who may have been taught the wrong coping methods, has the wrong perspective and was trained to view others and themselves in the wrong light. This person may have been taught the wrong way to deal with conflict, and they face a myriad of internal struggles on top of the many external problems they already have. They have layers and layers of issues, and so do you.

Problems are an opportunity to create greater intimacy between you and your partner. They should not be seen as the wall in the way of true intimacy between the two of you, but rather, they should be seen as the bridge to your partner's soul. People love and appreciate the individuals that help them to face and overcome their demons. That is how greater intimacy is built in a relationship. It's built not through secrecy but transparency; it's built when you let your guard down and allow another to enter into your world to witness all of the pain and scars left upon your heart by trials and tribulations, and vice-versa.

You're in your partner's life to help them heal, and they're in your life to help you heal. The intimacy in your relationship will come to a halt when you or your partner pretends not to have an area that requires healing and improvement. Intimacy requires vulnerability. Vulnerability requires honesty, humility, and openness. Being vulnerable means you've taken the chance to open up the door of your heart to someone else, allowing them to get close enough to you to affect you on a level deeper than anyone else ever could, which is the ultimate expression of trust.

Sure, you can get hurt by that person, but you can also have your life transformed positively by them. You're taking a chance whenever you open up your heart to love. When God guides your steps and pairs you with the individual He wants you to be with, you are not risking your heart into deceitful and destructive hands, but rather, you're placing your heart into the hands of a vessel God intends to use to bring about much-needed healing in your life. That's why I can't overstate the importance of praying to God for His best and waiting for Him to send you the right partner. Trusting Him will save you a lot of heartache and pain.

HOLDING YOUR MAN ACCOUNTABLE

Now ladies, let me remind you that you're not in your man's life to play God and shape him into what you want him to be; you're in his life to help him first remain accountable to God. Remember that only God has the power to mend a broken heart and heal a wounded soul. Kind and loving words of affirmation help him in his journey; they help him when he's in a state of distress. He feels good knowing you're on his side, but ultimately, what he needs to be reminded of is that God is for him. God can

CHAPTER 5: EVERY MAN NEEDS ACCOUNTABILITY

do for him what you or any other person can't do; this is where your skill as a man's wife and companion gets put to the test. You may not want to hear this part, but often it takes a woman to draw a man to God. It's funny that in the Old Testament, whenever Satan wanted to draw a man away from God, he'd use a woman to do it: Eve, Delilah, Jezebel, Solomon's seven-hundred, and the list continues. And just like the devil used a woman to lure Adam away from God, God used a woman to restore man to God (Genesis 3:15). God brought eternal reconciliation into the world through a teenage girl named Mary. And He continues to use women to execute His plan on Earth through women. He saved the entire Jewish nation through a woman named Esther. He led the nation of Israel through one of its darkest seasons through a woman named Deborah. He used a woman named Lydia to finance the Apostle Paul's ministry when many churches were struggling to do so. He used a woman to alert the disciples of Jesus' resurrection. And I can go on and on with this. But the point is simple: You may be the only bridge between that man and God, which is why there's so much pressure and responsibility on you as the wife. That is what 1 Peter 3:1 emphasizes so strongly. A preacher won't persuade an unbelieving, hard-hearted, stubborn, non-God-fearing husband. A track, program he sees on television, someone knocking on his door in the morning, or some other means won't persuade him. He'll most likely be "won over by the conversation of the wives" (the word "conversation" means "manner of life, conduct, behavior, deportment" in the Greek language). So the way you handle him can either propel him towards God or deter him from God. Of course, he has to take personal responsibility for the state of his soul, but your witness in the home plays a crucial part in his spiritual development.

Helping your man to become and remain accountable to God doesn't mean preaching to him, and it doesn't mean criticizing his weaknesses and condemning him for his mistakes. Quite the opposite. That's why Peter emphasized that you let your attitude, behavior, respect, gentle and meek spirit do the preaching. Let him fall in love with the incredible woman you are or are becoming, and then he'll become more drawn to the God who's performed or is causing such a transformation in your life. Whereas you used to snap and lose your temper, call him out of his name and disrespect him, now you're honoring him and treating him with respect, even though he may not deserve it. He'll begin to wonder why you're honoring him so much and treating him with so much respect when he knows he's unworthy of it. Of course, this is because you've learned what the Bible teaches about all of us doing our part as individuals in the relationship. You've discovered that God tells the husband to love his wife not because she treats him right but because this honors God. Likewise, the wife respects and honor her husband not if he acts like a man worthy of honor and respect, but simply because she is honoring God by doing so. As the Apostle Paul noted in Colossians 3:18-25,

> "Wives, submit yourselves to your husbands, as is fitting in the Lord. Husbands, love your wives and do not be harsh with them. Children, obey your parents in everything, for this pleases the Lord. Fa-

CHAPTER 5: EVERY MAN NEEDS ACCOUNTABILITY

thers, do not embitter your children, or they will become discouraged. [Servants], obey your earthly masters in everything; and do it, not only when their eye is on you and to curry their favor, but with sincerity of heart and reverence for the Lord. Whatever you do, work at it with all your heart, as working for the Lord, not for human masters, since you know that you will receive an inheritance from the Lord as a reward. It is the Lord Christ you are serving. Anyone who does wrong will be repaid for their wrongs, and there is no favoritism."

Your respect and submission to your husband aren't based on fear and manipulation; it is a choice of yours based on your service to God. You treat that man better than he deserves because God loves and treats you better than you deserve, and you want to please Him. That takes the ego out of the equation and causes your motives for serving your spouse to be pure. And purity of heart is what you're going to need to be the wife that man needs in his life.

In her bestselling book *The Power of a Praying Wife*, Stormie Omartian explains the power of a praying wife. She describes how a wife's prayers have a greater effect on him than anyone else's actions, but the key to her prayers being heard and answered by God is that she must maintain a pure heart before God first. Stormie writes,

> "The hard part about being a praying wife, other than the sacrifice of time, is maintaining a pure heart. It must be clean before God in order for

you to see good results. That's why praying for a husband must begin with praying for his wife. If you have resentment, anger, unforgiveness, or an ungodly attitude—even if there's good reason for it—you'll have a difficult time seeing answers to your prayers. But if you can release those feelings to God in total honesty and then move into prayer, there is nothing that can change a marriage more dramatically."

She goes on to explain how to process and handle negative emotions towards your spouse so that your heart can remain pure before God in this passage:

"I Don't Even Like Him—How Can I Pray for Him? Have you ever been so mad at your husband that the last thing you wanted to do was pray for him? So have I. It's hard to pray for someone when you're angry or he's hurt you. But that's exactly what God wants us to do. If He asks us to pray for our enemies, how much more should we be praying for the person with whom we have become one and are supposed to love? But how do we get past the unforgiveness and critical attitude? The first thing to do is be completely honest with God. In order to break down the walls in our hearts and smash the barriers that stop communication, we have to be totally up-front with the Lord about our feelings. We don't have to 'pretty it up' for Him. He already knows the truth. He just wants to see if we're willing to admit it and confess it as

CHAPTER 5: EVERY MAN NEEDS ACCOUNTABILITY

disobedience to His ways."

Yes, as a wife, as a companion, you play the biggest part in a man's life. You are in that man's life not to play God but to lead him to God through your godly behavior and lifestyle. That is why you must first become accountable to God. Do this and watch what happens. Watch and see if that man starts to change and spend more time with God. Sometimes, you have to empower him to become the priest of the home before he takes on the confidence to become the priestly leader in the household. Be patient.

PERSONAL ACCOUNTABILITY

Praying for your man is one of the greatest things you can do for him; it's what changes his heart and redirects his path. But be also prepared for God to hold your feet to the fire as well. One of the biggest aspects of accountability in marriage and relationships is the willingness to take responsibility for your actions. In other words, avoid the blame game and immediately apologize whenever you're the one in the wrong.

Joyce Myers once stated, those three words ("I am sorry") have saved more marriages than anything else. Taking responsibility for our actions demonstrates a level of emotional maturity often missing in many relationships; it reveals to our partners that we are willing to change and to grow along with them. When we confess to our wrongs and own up to them, we display a level of vulnerability that is attractive and reassuring to our partners. They begin to feel less judged by us and more accepted by us.

5 THINGS EVERY MAN NEEDS

Turn off the television. Put the cell phone down. Tell the kids to go to bed early, and then take your husband by the hands, look him in the eyes, and remind him of why you are there: that you are a partner who's come alongside him on this golden-brick road of personal development. Both of you are on your way to see the Wiz (in this case, the Heavenly Father, the one who knows the secrets of all men's hearts and can heal every wound in our souls). Let your man know that when he hurts, you hurt. Open up to him and let him know how much you appreciate him being in your life—how he's helped you grow in your journey towards becoming a better woman, how much he's contributed to your life and how God has used him to be a blessing to you. Allow your transparency and vulnerability with one another to take your relationship deeper than it's ever gone and establish a level of intimacy you may not have thought possible. That's what he wants more than anything else. That's what he needs. And not only him, but you, too.

ABOUT THE AUTHOR

Pastor Dwight Kevin Buckner, Jr, affectionately known on social media as Pastor Dwight, is a proud husband, father, pastor and man of God. Widely known from his appearances on the hit Lifetime reality show, *Married at First Sight*. Buckner is the special relationship advisor

Buckner has a long history of time spent in the church and growing under the leadership of other senior pastors. Buckner was born in Minneapolis, Minnesota to Pastor Dwight Kevin Buckner, Sr. and Angela Buckner. He comes from a Pentecostal background and proudly upholds the family tradition of pastoring and being a servant to the church. Buckner is a seventh generation pastor. Under the leadership of his great uncle, Dr. Walter L. Battle, who was the pastor of the Gospel Temple C.O.G.I.C Church in St. Paul, Minnesota. Following the long-lasting legacy of family in ministry, Buckner began to realize the call to preach God's word at 16 years-old.

After confirmation of the call to preach Buckner started to prepare to step into his destiny. In 2004 he enrolled in Beulah Heights Bible College in Atlanta, GA and graduated with a B.A. in Leadership Administration in May of 2007. Buckner was later ordained and licensed as a Minister of the Gospel in December of 2009. Buckner later decided to continue his education at the Pentecostal Seminary in Cleveland, Tennessee, earning a Master of Divinity degree.

Buckner founded and currently serves as senior pastor at Generation of Hope Church in Decatur, GA. He works diligently to reach at-risk youth, young adults, broken families, and most of all people unfamiliar with the church, around the world. Buckner is also an entrepreneur and author of the book *Breaking the Cycle of Lust*, which was his first book. He is a national public speaker and relationship advisor currently available for media inquiries and speaking opportunities.

Buckner resides in Atlanta, GA with his wife, Elisa Bennett Buckner and two children, Elias Dwight Buckner and Malachi Caleb Buckner.

All media and booking inquiries should be directed to PRTeam@epimediagroup.com